RADAR

AND THE RAFT

A True Story About a Scientific Marvel, the Lives It Saved, and the World It Changed

Jeff Lantos

Charlesbridge

For my dad, Raymond Lantos, who landed with the second wave on Omaha Beach, June 6, 1944

Published by Charlesbridge
9 Galen Street
Watertown, MA 02472
(617) 926-0329 • www.charlesbridge.com

Library of Congress Cataloging-in-Publication Data
Names: Lantos, Jeff, author.
Title: Radar and the raft: a true story about a scientific marvel, the lives it saved, and the world it changed / Jeff Lantos.
Description: Watertown, MA: Charlesbridge, 2024. | Includes bibliographical references and index. | Audience: Ages 10 and up | Audience: Grades 4–6 | Summary: "Follow two storylines—one about the scientific discoveries that led to the creation of radar, the other about people stranded on a raft in WWII—that come together when radar finds the raft." —Provided by publisher.
Identifiers: LCCN 2023032155 (print) | LCCN 2023032156 (ebook) | ISBN 9781623543457 (hardcover) | ISBN 9781632893109 (ebook)
Subjects: LCSH: World War, 1939–1945—Radar—Juvenile literature. | Radar—History—Juvenile literature. | West Lashaway (Cargo ship)—Juvenile literature. | Bell family—Juvenile literature. | Shipwrecks—Atlantic Ocean—Juvenile literature. | Shipwreck survival—Atlantic Ocean—Juvenile literature. | Search and rescue operations--Atlantic Ocean—History—Juvenile literature. | World War, 1939–1945—Atlantic Ocean—Juvenile literature.
Classification: LCC D810.R33 L368 2024 (print) | LCC D810.R33 (ebook) | DDC 940.54/5—dc23/eng/20230909
LC record available at https://lccn.loc.gov/2023032155
LC ebook record available at https://lccn.loc.gov/2023032156

Printed in China
(hc) 10 9 8 7 6 5 4 3 2 1

Illustrations done in watercolor inks on Fabriano 5 paper
Display type set in Hitch Route by BoxTube Labs and LeHavre by Jeremy Dooley
Text type set in Arno Pro by Adobe Systems Incorporated
Printed by 1010 Printing International Limited in Huizhou, Guangdong, China
Production supervision by Mira Kennedy
Designed by Diane M. Earley

CONTENTS

CAST OF CHARACTERS

THE SCIENTISTS

André-Marie Ampère, French
Henry A. H. Boot, English
Edward Bowen, English
Karl Braun, German
Martin Cooper, American
Michael Faraday, English
Luigi Galvani, Italian
Heinrich Hertz, German
Immanuel Kant, German
Guglielmo Marconi, Italian
James Clerk Maxwell, Scottish
Isaac Newton, English
Hans Christian Oersted, Danish
Robert M. Page, American
Eugene Polley, American
John T. Randall, English
Percy Spencer, American
Albert Hoyt Taylor, American
Nikola Tesla, Serbian American

Alessandro Volta, Italian
Robert Watson-Watt, Scottish
Leo Young, American

THE RAFTERS

Ethel Bell, civilian passenger
Mary Bell, civilian passenger, age 13
Robert Bell, civilian passenger, age 11
Benjamin Bogdan, merchant marine captain
Joseph Greenwell, merchant marine first assistant engineer
Frank S. Flavor, merchant marine utility
Earl "Flags" Koonz, US Navy Reserve seaman second class
George Marano, merchant marine fireman
Robert McDaniel, merchant marine messman
Isabelino Pacheco, merchant marine ordinary seaman
James Peifer, merchant marine boatswain (bosun)
Woodman Ray Potter, merchant marine second cook
C. J. Rosibrosiris, merchant marine chief cook
Servior Seramos, merchant marine able seaman
Carol Shaw, civilian passenger, age 7
Richard Shaw, civilian passenger, age 13
John Vargas, merchant marine pantryman and baker
Louis G. Vega, merchant marine oiler
Levi Walker, merchant marine messman

ANY SUFFICIENTLY ADVANCED TECHNOLOGY
IS INDISTINGUISHABLE FROM MAGIC.
—Arthur C. Clarke, author

I SHALL PRAY FOR RADAR AND TRUST IN GOD.
—Hugh "Stuffy" Dowding, British air marshal

HELL IS A LONG NIGHT ON A CROWDED RAFT.
—Robert Bell, eleven-year-old survivor

PROLOGUE

SUMMER 1942. World War II rages. On one side are Germany, Italy, and Japan (the Axis powers). On the other side are the United States, Great Britain, and Russia (the Allies).

German dictator Adolf Hitler has already seized much of Europe, and to the east a German invasion force battles Russian fighters in what is now Ukraine. Hitler's ally Japan has taken over the Philippines, the Dutch East Indies (now Indonesia), Malaysia, and Burma (now Myanmar). Hitler's other ally, Italy, occupies western Egypt, British Somaliland (now Somalia), and much of Greece. German submarines (called U-boats) prowl the Atlantic Ocean and the Mediterranean Sea torpedoing hundreds of American and British cargo ships and oil tankers. Japanese submarines wreak the same havoc in the Pacific Ocean. All around the globe, white-knuckle scenes of life and death play out on land, in the air, and on the seas.

One of these scenes is unfolding in the South Atlantic, several hundred miles northeast of Venezuela. Under a relentless sun, a wooden life raft—ten feet long and eight feet wide—is seesawing over the ocean swells. Kept afloat by six forty-two-gallon steel cans called drums, the raft rides three feet above the water. There's a splintery plank seat around the inside perimeter. Water sloshes through gaps in the slats at the bottom of the raft.

Crammed into the eighty square feet are seventeen glassy-eyed Americans. Nine days earlier, there were nineteen people on the raft, but two have died. Of those remaining, twelve are merchant marines, four are children, and one is an adult named Ethel Bell. She's the mother of two of the children: Mary Bell, age thirteen, and Robert Bell, age eleven.

The raft has been drifting westward for more than two weeks. Food and water supplies are running low. The rafters spend their waking hours squinting at the sea and sky, hoping to glimpse a passing ship or a low-flying plane.

These seventeen people will end up surviving only because their rescuers are aided by a new sensing device called radar. That name was coined just two years earlier, in 1940. It's an acronym plucked from the words "radio detection and ranging."

Robert, Mary, Ethel, and their raftmates are not the first people rescued by this new secret weapon. They certainly won't be the last. In addition to helping with search-and-rescue operations

TORPEDO TRANSPORT

U-boat is short for the German word *Unterseeboot*, meaning "under the sea boat." Despite the name, U-boats spent most of their time on the surface and submerged only to escape an enemy or to mount a rare daytime attack. In 1942, German U-boats carried fifteen torpedoes. Six were carefully slid directly into the U-boat's launch tubes. The others were stored in lower bunks (underneath dozing sailors) or in a specially designed compartment between the upper and lower levels of the vessel. While a boat was at sea, torpedoes had to be serviced every few days. Technicians recharged batteries and made sure nothing had been contaminated by salt water. Once a torpedo was fired, crewmen reloaded the empty tube. U-boat captains were expected to fire all torpedoes before returning to port.

during World War II, radar played a vital role in locating and tracking enemy planes, ships, and U-boats before they could deliver lethal attacks. Knowing where the enemy is and where they're going is usually a prelude to victory. Indeed, the scientists and engineers who built the American and British radar systems became convinced that radar, more than any other weapon, made possible the Allied victory over the Axis powers in World War II.

Following the war, radar technology was used to produce a multitude of new devices, several of which are likely in your house. One may be in your backpack right now. When it comes to changing the world, radar ranks right up there with the printing press, the electric light, the automobile, the airplane, and the computer. So how did radar become a reality? And under what circumstances did a British navy man use it to find a little raft full of people in the South Atlantic?

Get ready to dive into two intertwining stories. In one thread, you'll meet a small group of international scientists who step by step and decade by decade unraveled some of nature's deepest secrets. Like relay runners, they passed their findings from one person to the next until December 1934, when two Americans—Leo Young and Robert Page—built and demonstrated the world's first true radar set at the US Naval Research Laboratory in Washington, DC.

In the other story, you'll meet an unlikely group of rafters brought together by warfare's indiscriminate savagery: nineteen resolute souls, most of whom were able to cheat death thanks to the miracle of electromagnetic radiation.

Let's begin with a question: How did the two Bell kids and their mom wind up on a sunbaked raft in the vast ocean in the middle of a world war?

CHAPTER 1
OFF TO AFRICA

ROBERT BELL was a third grader at Upper Nyack Elementary School, about thirty-five miles north of New York City, in 1938. Because he lived only a few blocks from the school, he could hear the first morning bell from his kitchen table. Three more spoonfuls of Rice Krispies and a sprint along his special shortcut put Robert in his seat by the time the second bell rang at eight forty-five. His sister, Mary, was in the fifth grade. She was not as daring as her brother and was already at her desk reading a book as Robert was still munching.

Their recently widowed mother, Ethel, was a Christian missionary who at age forty-five had already completed several two-year assignments in the West African country of French Sudan (now Mali). Her late husband, George, also a missionary, had been returning home from a tour of churches in New England when his bus collided with a truck in the middle of the night.

Mary had run home from school that day eager to see her father after his long trip. She opened the door and called, "Daddy!" but there was no answer. "I went from room to room," she said, "and finally came to the back bedroom; there I found Mother sitting alone with the shades drawn. 'Daddy isn't coming home,' she said. 'He's gone to heaven.'"

Robert was barely five at the time and had a limited memory of his father. He did recall once being spanked for disobedience, but afterward his father held Robert on his lap, told him he loved him, and made sure his son understood why he had been punished. He was a "loving father," said Robert, "fair but firm."

George and Ethel had intended to continue their missionary work in West Africa. Ethel told her pastor that she was determined to adhere to that plan, and that God's presence would help her through her grief. The pastor wasn't so sure that West Africa was the best place for a widow and two young children. Ethel wasn't deterred. She said that after George's death, it seemed as if the Lord had reached down, grabbed her hand, and whispered words from Isaiah 41:10: "Be not dismayed, for I am thy God. I will strengthen thee, yea, I will help thee." Even with the Bible's help, it still took her two years to convince the pastor and the mission board that she was ready. They finally gave approval in the spring of 1938 and assigned Mrs. Bell to a new station in Bouaké, Ivory Coast.

When the school year ended in June, the three Bells packed up and got yellow fever and diphtheria vaccinations and vials of pills to prevent malaria and dysentery. Saying goodbye to friends and family wasn't easy, but both kids were excited about heading to the bustling New York waterfront, boarding a big ocean liner, and sailing off to West Africa.

It's easy to picture Ethel and Robert standing at the ship's rail, staring at the sparkling Manhattan skyline, and just as easy to imagine Mary opening a guidebook and showing off her reading skills. Guidebooks at the time might've said something like this: *Ivory Coast (or Cote d'Ivoire) is named for its most famous export, although overhunting of elephants collapsed the West African ivory trade around 1910. The Portuguese were the first Europeans to sail along the Ivory Coast in 1482. Dutch and French explorers followed, and the French were the first to establish a mission there, in 1687. Over the next 150 years, French missionaries, traders, and soldiers arrived, and in the 1840s the French signed a series of treaties with local West African chiefs that allowed France to construct fortified posts along the Gulf of Guinea to serve as permanent trading centers. The official language is French, but over seventy regional languages are also spoken.*

A deafening blare from the ship's horn would have interrupted Mary's history lesson. Dockworkers lifted the thick mooring lines off the iron cleats, the big engines revved, and black smoke rose from the two stacks. The six-hundred-foot-long Cunard liner *Laconia* eased its way into the Hudson River and floated south past Battery Park and the Statue of Liberty. It sailed through Upper Bay and Lower Bay and then took an eastward turn and gained a bit more speed along the length of Long Island from Long Beach to Montauk before gliding into the open sea.

With the *Laconia* calling at many ports along the way, it was three months before the Bells finally disembarked in Abidjan, the largest city in Ivory Coast, with a population around 180,000. After a night in a hotel, they rode a train more than two hundred miles north to Bouaké. This being a new missionary post, there was no

RMS Laconia, circa 1921

school for foreign children. The nearest such school was not in a nearby village or town, but in the neighboring country of Guinea. A chaperone/driver picked up Mary and Robert and their suitcases and took them on a two-day, seven-hundred-mile road trip to the Guinean city of Mamou, where they boarded with a local French-speaking couple. It didn't take long for the young Americans to pick up the new language, and within a month or so they were able to have conversations with their friendly hosts, who had no children of their own. When Robert and Mary were together, they flipped from French to English. Perhaps they picked up some favorite French gestures: Mary kissing and spreading her fingers as she says *"Magnifique"* or *"Délicieuse."* Robert tapping one side of his nose with his index finger and saying *"J'ai du pif,"* meaning *I've got the nose for it* when he knew something already.

The Statue of Liberty in New York Harbor

After their classes, Robert and the other white schoolboys (from the United States and Canada) played all their games with the African boys, and it got Robert wondering why at home only white men played major league baseball. It would be several more years before he understood the words *segregation* and *discrimination*.

Mary and Robert rarely spoke about missing their mom. Sure, they probably would have liked more mom hugs and bedtime stories, but how could they complain? They knew she was doing what she believed was important work—bringing Christian biblical teachings to people all over the globe.

When the school year ended in June 1939, the missionary kids scattered for the summer. Robert, Mary, and Ethel were able to enjoy some family time in Ivory Coast before the kids returned to Mamou again in late August. On September 2, 1939, shocking news crackled over the radio. The day before, Hitler had sent a massive German invasion force into Poland, where they crushed the unprepared and outgunned Polish fighters. Honoring an alliance made with Poland six months earlier, Great Britain and France both declared war on Germany on September 3. Great Britain also announced a blockade of Germany. In response, Hitler unleashed air and sea attacks on British and French warships, merchant vessels, and submarines in the North Sea and English Channel. World War II had begun. For the next six months, most of the fighting took place on the sea or in the sky.

UNHAPPY ENDING

Four years after the Bells' journey, the Laconia was sunk by a U-boat off the coast of West Africa. Of the 2,732 crew, passengers, soldiers, and Italian prisoners of war aboard, roughly 1,000 were rescued.

But in May 1940, after the snow had melted and the roads dried out, Hitler's tanks and trucks rolled westward into France, Belgium, Luxembourg, and the Netherlands. In none of these countries was the army able to slow or stop the powerful and fast-moving German war machine. Luxembourg surrendered in one day, the Netherlands in less than a week, Belgium soon after, and France the following month.

French capitulation meant that Guinea, Ivory Coast, and the six other French colonies in West Africa were suddenly under Hitler's control. Not long afterward, German soldiers arrived in West Africa, and government buildings were adorned with huge banners featuring the symbol of Hitler's Nazi party, the swastika.

How did the United States react to all this? First consider the history. Only twenty-five years earlier, in 1914, World War I began. Over thirty countries were eventually involved in the conflict, but the main combatants were France and Britain (the Allies) on one side, and Germany and Austria-Hungary (the Central Powers) on the other. After three years of warfare, the outcome was still in doubt. In 1917, the United States entered the war on the side of the Allies. It was the sudden infusion of American troops and weaponry that tipped the balance and forced German leaders to surrender and sign a peace treaty in 1919. One provision of that treaty prohibited Germany from manufacturing new weapons of war. But almost from the start, German leaders defied the treaty and the country's military began covertly rearming itself. In 1939 and 1940, with Germany once again attacking and occupying neighboring countries, President Franklin Delano Roosevelt faced a difficult decision. Should he urge Congress to declare war on Germany, or should the United States try to remain neutral? In July 1940, this choice became more difficult when the newly appointed prime minister of Britain, Winston Churchill, wrote to President Roosevelt asking for military assistance. That was the first of many such requests. At the same time, plenty of influential Americans (such as aviator Charles Lindbergh and Ambassador to London Joseph Kennedy) urged President Roosevelt to avoid getting the nation involved in another European war. Master politician that he was, Roosevelt found a way to please both sides. He sent vital food, oil, and military equipment to the United Kingdom, but he kept American soldiers and sailors at home.

Hitler meanwhile reached out to two fellow autocrats, Prime Minister Benito Mussolini in Italy and Emperor Hirohito in Japan. In September 1940, these three signed the Tripartite Pact, which promised retaliation by all three countries if the United States entered the war.

Back in Ivory Coast, Mrs. Bell felt that as long as the United States remained neutral, it was safe to leave her children in Guinea to continue their schooling. And it was safe—until Emperor Hirohito and his Japanese military leaders made a brazen decision. Without consulting Hitler, they ordered a surprise attack on the United States.

On December 7, 1941, a few minutes after six o'clock in the morning, 353 Japanese planes took off from six aircraft carriers in the Pacific Ocean. Two hours later these fighter planes and bombers pummeled the US naval base at Pearl Harbor in Hawaii. Over twenty-four hundred Americans were killed, eighteen ships sunk or run aground, and over three hundred airplanes damaged or destroyed. The next day, the United States Congress declared war on Japan. Three days later, Hitler proclaimed that Germany would support Japan, and he declared war on the United States. A few hours after the German declaration, President Roosevelt rushed a "war message" to Congress. He stressed the need to confront this threat to life, liberty, and civilization, and he warned that "delay invites greater danger." Congress didn't delay. It declared war on Germany. The vote was 88–0 in the Senate and 393–0 in the House.

Suddenly it was no longer safe to hold an American passport in Nazi-controlled French West Africa. Mrs. Bell made immediate arrangements for her children to be brought back to Bouaké by rail and car. As soon as they arrived, she began to look for a way out of Ivory Coast. To leave the country, American citizens needed French exit visas. But with German occupiers now in charge of French immigration officials, this would be no easy matter.

Mrs. Bell wrote, "There were many negotiations to be entered into, a multitude of letters to be written, interviews with French officials to be carried on, and all the time, hopes and fears fluctuated . . . one had to be possessed of great patience in those days." Several times—in March, April, and again in May—Mrs. Bell thought she was about to secure the necessary papers. Then would come some hitch, flimsy excuse, or shake of a head.

On June 12, the Bells were officially denied permission to leave Ivory Coast. They were in effect trapped behind enemy lines. What now?

DON'T BLAME RADAR

Why didn't American radar operators detect Japanese bombers approaching Pearl Harbor? Answer: They did! At 7:02 on the morning of December 7, at the US Army radar station on Oahu, Private George E. Elliott saw a blip at a range of 140 miles. His partner, Private Joseph Lockhard, said it "was the biggest reflection [he] had ever seen at such a range." The planes were flying straight at them. Lockhard placed a call to First Lieutenant Kermit A. Tyler. Like his commanding officers, Tyler believed that Hawaii would not be attacked by air. He had heard that a squadron of American B-17 bombers was scheduled to pass on its way to the Philippines, so he told the radar men not to worry. The attack began less than an hour later, at 7:55 a.m.

*Newspapers around the country announced
that the United States had entered the war*

CHAPTER 2

ESCAPE

THE BELLS GOT LUCKY. A Frenchman in the consular office finally decided that Mrs. Bell had endured enough stress and torment. Catching up to her one day as she exited the building, the man offered to help Mrs. Bell and her children flee to the neighboring British colony of Gold Coast (today called Ghana).

The easiest way to travel from Bouaké to the western border of Gold Coast was to take one train south to Abidjan and another train a hundred miles east to the border. But that route was out of the question because the train stations in Bouaké and Abidjan were patrolled by German soldiers and their local minions. The Germans had also increased security at highway crossings between Ivory Coast and Gold Coast. The man at the consular office told Mrs. Bell that without exit papers her only option was a roundabout, weeks-long, four-hundred-mile trip through two countries. He offered to drive the Bells on the first leg of the journey. Mrs. Bell didn't hesitate. Departure was scheduled for the wee hours of June 16, 1942. While waiting for the car, the Bells filled their canteens with water and their pockets with dried fruit.

As promised, the Frenchman picked up the Bells and drove them twenty-five miles north to the town of Katiola, where in the predawn darkness the Americans thanked their courageous benefactor and boarded a train heading north. Mary wrote that this "was the beginning of what we children thought was a super adventure."

After 150 miles, the train neared the northern border of Ivory Coast. No exit papers were demanded or examined here because the train was crossing into another German-controlled French colony called Upper Volta (now Burkina Faso). Another hundred miles brought the Bells to the city of Bobo-Dioulasso. Though we don't know for sure, it's likely the compassionate Frenchman had told Mrs. Bell what sort of person to seek out at the train station and what code word to say when she approached him. This contact must have been a truck driver, because Mary wrote, "From 'Bobo' we rode atop baggage on a truck to [the capital city of] Ouagadougou." Here Mrs. Bell once again had to write letters, fill out forms, smile at supercilious French and German officials, and endure several weeks of bureaucratic rigamarole.

Some local Nazi-haters came to the rescue. First a slight, chain-smoking man in the French consular office walked past his boss's desk, deftly palmed the official stamper, and pressed the inky imprint onto Mrs. Bell's papers. When he handed her the documents, he whispered that the Bells should be ready to leave early the next morning.

"We left town before dawn," wrote Mary, "because the French didn't want the Nazis to catch them helping us." Their route took them over unmapped dirt roads, across bridgeless streams, and past a Gurunsi village. Drinking water was scarce, their truck was creaky, and lingering over the entire enterprise was the constant fear of being stopped, interrogated, and turned back.

As they neared the border of Gold Coast, Mrs. Bell could feel her heartbeat quickening. The truck eased up to a traffic arm and a guardhouse. An armed soldier emerged and demanded exit papers. Mrs. Bell handed them to the driver, who handed them to the soldier. The children watched. The driver stared straight ahead. Mrs. Bell reminded herself to breathe. The soldier flipped through the papers, peered into the truck, and looked again at the papers. He handed them back to the driver, turned, and walked back into the guardhouse. The traffic arm rose, and the truck rolled forward.

"What a relief it was at last to cross the frontier," wrote Mrs. Bell. "To see flying from the flagpole the Union Jack that told us no power could lay claim to us or prevent our going on our journey."

British authorities pampered the Bells. They not only provided transportation by lorry and train to Accra, 375 miles away; they also booked rooms for them at the Metropole, a fancy hotel that featured a tiled lobby, hand-decorated ceilings, carved wooden hangers, a gilt elevator with a wrought-iron door, and rooms that overlooked the Gulf of Guinea. From the hotel, Mrs. Bell sent a Western Union telegram to the Christian and Missionary Alliance headquarters in New York, briefing them on the situation and requesting hotel and travel funds. That money arrived electronically at the Accra Western Union office two days later, the same day the Bells celebrated Robert's eleventh birthday: July 20, 1942.

"Mother found someone at the hotel to bake me a birthday cake," wrote Robert, "and we had my favorite meal, roast beef and gravy, mashed potatoes and peas." The next day Mrs. Bell began looking for a way to get the three of them back to New York.

The first thing she discovered was that a month earlier the Americans had established an air base in Accra, but all the planes flew war materials to the British Eighth Army based in Cairo, Egypt. It was this emergency airlift that enabled the British and their Australian and New Zealand allies to halt the German and Italian offensive. By winning this battle (near the town of El-Alamein), they prevented the Germans and Italians from advancing across Egypt and seizing the strategically important Suez Canal. As for ships, most of those carried war materials and captured German equipment rather than ordinary passengers. "Everything was tied into the war effort," wrote Robert. To make matters worse, Accra was full of thousands of frightened foreigners all trying to get home from North Africa and the Middle East.

At the office of Pan American Airways, Mrs. Bell asked for three seats on one of the westbound planes called Stratoliners that flew from Accra to New York with multiple refueling stops: in Ascension Island in the South Atlantic; Natal, Brazil; and Miami, Florida. The clerk told her that the few available seats on outgoing flights were reserved for military or government personnel, and he encouraged her to consider traveling by cargo ship. Mrs. Bell hiked down to the wharf, introduced herself to the port agent, and put her family's names on a waiting list. A week went by. No one called. July turned to August. Still no call.

The funny thing was the Bell children didn't mind being stranded. "Mary and I had a great time in Accra," wrote Robert. There were no classes to attend, the beach was close, the sand was

Mrs. Bell hoped she could get tickets to fly home on this type of plane

soft, the water was clear and warm, and the days were long. Every street corner sported a kiosk where you could buy cold drinks and listen to American jazz and swing music on a gramophone. Just blocks from the hotel was an outdoor market unlike any the Bell kids had ever seen: a block-long maze of vendors hawking flowing fabrics, beaded jewelry, bubu robes, handwoven baskets, braided leather sandals, hats, socks, earrings, handbags, water jugs, soccer balls, board games, car parts, fish, chickens, snails, onions, okra, eggplant, peppers, kola nuts, and melons of every size and color. The saleswomen smiled, shouted, and beckoned; the monkeys screeched; the kingfishers squawked; and the bongo players pounded away. Lunch was always a treat. Baked yams, fried tilapia, calaloo (savory vegetable stew), fufu (boiled cassava and plantains), aloko (fried plantains), and melon fingers with lime, all washed down with ice-cold Coca-Cola.

There were a few reminders of the fighting in Europe, Asia, and North Africa: headlines in newspapers, newsreels in movie

theaters, and a sunken cargo ship in the shallow water of the harbor—the victim of a German U-boat.

"I could have stayed in Accra forever," wrote Robert. His mom felt differently. She worried that Accra might become a target of Germany or Italy. These fears were not unfounded. A German plane had already dropped sixteen bombs on an allied fort in the central African country of Chad, German prisoners of war were brought to Ivory Coast to build a U-boat base, and every night a radio station in Abidjan blasted Nazi propaganda into Gold Coast.

The first week of August passed. On August 8, Mrs. Bell went down to the shipping office and made another plea to the port agent, who said he expected cargo ships to arrive at either Accra or the nearby port of Takoradi in the next few days. He promised to call the hotel as soon as he heard anything.

The Bells took their usual afternoon "stroll around the streets of Accra" and found an aromatic food stand near Korle Lagoon, site of the first settlement in Accra and home to fish, shrimp, crabs, and the meaty African tiger frog, the most popular edible frog in the area.

Here we can make a surprising connection: 150 years before the Bells arrived in Gold Coast, another edible frog led a scientist to draw a startling conclusion—one that set in motion a series of experiments that would eventually lead to a lifesaving blip on a ship's radar screen in the South Atlantic.

ACCRA SWINGS!

After the United States entered World War II, American servicemen and contractors came to Accra, Gold Coast (now Ghana), with "wads of money." Young soldiers flocked to dance clubs. The Accra Orchestra and the Accra Rhythmic Orchestra incorporated jazz and swing tunes into their song lists. To facilitate the new sound, both orchestras eliminated violin sections and added more brass, guitars, and percussion. The Accra musicians soon mastered such jazz standards as Count Basie's "One O'Clock Jump," and Glenn Miller's "American Patrol." Local men not only listened to jazz on the radio, they also dressed in blue jeans and incorporated American expressions (such as "Okay, babe") into their everyday language.

Accra, Ghana: Wilbur de Paris and New Orleans Jazz Band give out with a foxtrot at the Lido

The monument of Luigi Galvani in Bologna, Italy, overlaid with a drawing of his frog-leg experiment

CHAPTER 3
CURRENT EVENTS

LUIGI GALVANI was born in Bologna, Italy, in 1737. His father was a wealthy goldsmith who sent his son to the city's finest schools. After earning university degrees in medicine, surgery, and philosophy, Galvani was hired as a professor of anatomy at the University of Bologna.

According to Galvani family lore, a flulike illness struck the professor's wife, Signora Lucia Galvani, in 1791. Her doctor conducted an examination and concluded that the cure was cups of piping-hot frog soup. The Galvanis' housekeeper hurried to the market and procured a dozen or so high-jumping amphibians. The signora dutifully sipped her daily doses of the sea-green broth and recovered before all the frogs had been plopped into the soup pot. So Professor Galvani did what any good anatomist would do: He took the remaining frogs to his lab, sliced them open, pinned back the flaps, and studied their insides. Then he hung the frog corpses on copper hooks; got out his sketch pad; and made illustrations of their organs, bones, and powerful leg muscles.

Galvani happened to hang one of the copper hooks on an iron balcony railing. That's when something amazing happened: one leg of the dead frog jerked upward. *Cosa diavolo?* (What on earth?) Was it a message from the spirits? Was the leg still alive? What had triggered the convulsion? Over the next few days, Galvani repeated the experiment with different frogs and got the same twitchy results.

He concluded that the leg movements were generated by some sort of fluid flowing from the frog's nerves to the muscles in its legs. This liquid path (or circuit) carried the nerve pulses to the frog's leg muscles, causing them to contract. In his written report, Galvani called the fluid "animal electricity," and he suspected it was "inherent in the animal itself."

At the nearby University of Pavia, physics professor Alessandro Volta read Galvani's report with great interest. You could say the report *galvanized* Volta to repeat his colleague's experiment. Using the same components—a lifeless frog, a copper hook, and an iron railing—Volta witnessed the same leg twitches. At first he agreed with Galvani's theory, but after careful consideration, Volta concluded that his colleague's explanation was flawed. Rather than producing electricity, Volta believed that the frog's nerves and muscles were *reacting* to it. In that case, where did the electricity come from? Volta surmised the current was generated by the contact of the two different metals: the copper of the hook and the iron of the railing. And the frog's salty bodily fluids were *conducting*, or guiding, the flow of electric current from the copper hook down to the frog's leg muscles. It was easy enough to test this theory of contact electrification. Atop his tongue, Volta placed slivers of two different metals—silver and zinc. If he was right, when the two metals touched, his salty saliva would act as a conductor, and he would feel an electric current tingling the tip of his tongue. Which is exactly what happened. Volta wrote, "These [tingling] sensations continued if the mutual contact of the two metals was maintained." Anyone with metal dental braces or a metal tooth filling who bites down on a piece of aluminum foil can testify to the power of this type of small electric shock.

Despite Volta's findings, fans of Galvani's "animal electricity" theory refused to admit defeat. To win over the Galvani crowd, Volta wondered if there might be a way to use two dissimilar metals and a salty solution to generate a *continuous* current rather than a temporary one. If he could do that, it would likely end the debate.

Like so many great thinkers, Volta took his cue from nature. On his dissecting table, he laid out a torpedo fish commonly caught in the coastal waters of the Mediterranean Sea. Like the electric eel, the torpedo fish was a creature capable of generating electricity and zapping its prey "incessantly and without intermission." The fish's "natural electric organ," as Volta called it, was comprised of vertical columns, each one tightly packed with partitions. Picture each column as a stack of pennies.

After making "detailed anatomical studies" of the torpedo fish, Volta was ready to assemble his metallic imitation. First he took sixteen metal discs, each about a half-inch thick and four inches in diameter. Eight of the discs were zinc, and eight were copper. Next he took a piece of cardboard and soaked it in a salt-water-and-vinegar solution. Volta cut eight circles from the soggy cardboard, each with the same diameter as the metal discs. To build his stack Volta started with a copper disc on the bottom, then a zinc disc, then a circle of the smelly cardboard. Seven times he repeated this—copper, zinc, smelly cardboard—until the tower was about nine inches high. After dipping his two index fingers into the salty solution, Volta touched the highest and lowest discs simultaneously, and . . . *Proprio quell oche speravo!* (Just what I was hoping!) Volta felt, as he put it, "a succession of small shocks resembling those occasioned by . . . a torpedo [fish] in a weak condition." He noted that this shocking action "could be repeated again and again, the pile apparently possessing within itself an indefinite power of recuperation."

Finally, Volta ran a copper wire from the zinc disc on top to the copper disc on the bottom. This gave the electric current a direct route and gave the pile "the singular property . . . of re-charging itself continually and spontaneously without any . . . intervals in its operations." On March 20, 1800, Volta reported that he had created the world's first continuous electric circuit.

Galvani didn't live long enough to read of Volta's discovery. He had died two years earlier.

The disagreement between the two great Italian scientists had always been respectful, and to honor his colleague, Volta coined the term *galvanism* to describe an electric jolt produced by a chemical reaction between two different metals. Three decades later scientists gave the name *galvanometer* to a new device that measured the strength of an electrical current.

As for Volta's tower of discs and cardboard, the best name he could come up with was "voltaic pile." Today you can find voltaic piles in nearly every home. Except they have a different name now: batteries. And on every package of batteries, you'll find the word *volt* or *voltage* or the abbreviation *V*, meaning the amount of electrical potential the battery holds.

In the world of science, unexpected discoveries (like twitching frog legs) usually lead to more unexpected discoveries. That's what occurred in 1820, when a Danish physicist named Hans Christian Oersted entered a lecture hall at the University of Copenhagen, built a voltaic pile, and then pulled a compass from his pocket. Why a compass? Because Professor Oersted wanted to see if there was any observable interaction between an electric current from the pile and the magnet in his compass.

An extra-tall voltaic pile created by Alessandro Volta.

At the time, most scientists considered electricity and magnetism to be distinct and unrelated phenomena. Oersted wasn't so sure. He knew that Benjamin Franklin had magnetized a needle by zapping it with electricity, and he knew that sea captains had reported wild fluctuations in their compasses during thunder and lightning storms. He also knew that both electricity and magnetism were influenced by opposing forces: positive and negative charges in the case of electricity, north and south poles in the case of magnetism. Oersted wasn't looking to explain the whys and wherefores of these two fundamental forces. He thought that such an explanation was likely beyond the reach of mortals. He was simply looking to see if one force had any effect on the other.

After generating an electric current, Oersted held his compass below the electrified wire. The magnetic needle in the compass jumped like Galvani's frog's leg had nearly thirty years earlier. *Du godeste! Vil du se på det?* (My goodness! Will you look at that?) When the needle stopped wiggling, it didn't return to its normal northward position. Instead it pointed east. When Oersted moved the compass above the live wire, the magnetic needle swung 180 degrees and pointed west. Not until Oersted cut the electric current did the compass needle return to its normal northward position.

Like any good scientist, Oersted had intended to conduct this experiment in the privacy of his lab, "but some accident . . . hindered him from trying it before the lecture." He could have canceled the lecture or changed topics, but he didn't. Instead he lugged his

ELECTRIFYING ARTIFACT

It turns out that Volta's pile may not have been the world's first battery. In 1938, German archeologist Wilhelm König was on a dig in Baghdad, Iraq, when he unearthed "an electrochemical cell made of copper and iron immersed in wine vinegar." This artifact, which has been dated to 250 BCE, has since been nicknamed the Baghdad Battery.

equipment into the lecture hall, set it up, and turned on the electric current. Only Oersted was close enough to see the quiver of the compass needle. When he looked up and told the audience what had just happened, no one seemed impressed. Only later would the attendees realize they had likely sat through the "only fundamental scientific discovery to have been made in front of an audience in a lecture hall."

So what happened here? Why did an electric current cause a compass needle to lose its bearings and point east and west instead of north?

It must be the case, Oersted wrote later, that when an electrical current is sent through a wire, the "electric conflict" isn't contained by the wire. Instead the current is "dispersed pretty widely" and it "performs circles" around the wire. Think of the live wire as the cardboard tube in the middle of a roll of paper towels. And think of the paper towels as the space into which the electric energy is dispersed.

But how would that space of electric energy disrupt a compass's normal operation? Oersted suspected that within an electric current there must also be some sort of magnetic power. Think about that: an electric current can not only tingle the tongue, it can

ENTERPRISING ELECTRONS

The discovery of electrons (in the 1890s) allowed scientists to understand why two dissimilar metals dipped in certain fluids produce an electric current. All matter is comprised of atoms, and inside each atom are smaller particles called electrons. Most electrons make regular orbits around the nucleus of their atom. But there are always a few electrons that stray. They're called "free electrons," and if given the chance, they'll jump from one atom to another. All they need to make that jump is a liquid form of transportation such as saliva, salt water, vinegar, or the gastric juices of a frog. When free electrons jump from, say, a silver atom to a zinc atom, that movement (or flow of electrons) is called electricity or electric current.

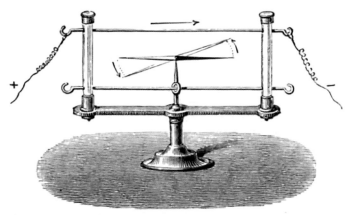

Hans Christian Oersted's experiment

also generate a magnetic force that overwhelms Earth's weaker magnetic force and flips a compass needle from vertical to horizontal.

Professor Oersted's account of his experiment was originally written in Latin and was sent to the most important science centers in Europe where it was "translated into German, French, and English and published in standard scientific journals." In France, scientist and mathematician André-Marie Ampère wrote, "From the very moment I have heard . . . of the beautiful discovery of M. Oersted at Copenhagen concerning the action of a current on the magnetic needle, I have continuously thought about it." He wasn't the only one. Oersted's experiment was "soon repeated in all countries in which there were friends of science."

We don't know whether Ethel Bell ever read or thought about Oersted's "beautiful discovery" in her high-school science classes. If so, she might have been aware that in her deluxe room at the Hotel Metropole in Accra she was surrounded by twentieth-century devices that depended on that same "action of a current on [a] magnetic needle." There was a ceiling fan that kept her cool at night, a reading light that illuminated her Bible, a radio that brought her news of American victories in the South Pacific, and most importantly a rotary telephone that finally rang on the morning of August 10.

CHAPTER 4
WESTWARD HO!

ON THE OTHER END of the ringing phone was the port agent. He said that in four days, an American cargo ship was due at Takoradi, 140 miles west of Accra. There was one vacant passenger room. Mrs. Bell booked it, and the family spent the day packing, buying souvenirs, and thanking the hotel staff. The next day they set off by bus. They had no worries on this trip since it was British territory all the way.

Right on schedule, the Seattle-built, 423-foot-long *West Lashaway* steamed into Takoradi. Owned by the New York–based Barber Steamship Lines, this was a workingman's freighter and a far cry from the luxurious ocean liner the Bells had boarded four years earlier.

The *West Lashaway* had stopped at several trading hubs along the west coast of Africa and was loaded with palm oil, latex, tin, manganese ore, cocoa beans, and (hang on to your hat!) fifty million dollars' worth of Congolese gold. Determined to keep this valuable resource from falling into Hitler's hands, two Frenchmen had met the *West Lashaway* in Matadi, the chief seaport in the Belgian Congo (now Democratic Republic of the Congo). Under cover of darkness, they had carted on board 1,900 pounds of gold. The gold was stashed in a giant lead safe in Captain Benjamin Bogdan's quarters, its presence known only to him and one officer. The Frenchmen had explained to Captain Bogdan how to get the gold back to Free France resistance fighters. These were the courageous men and women who sabotaged factories and blew up train tracks and bridges under the noses of the German occupation force. They also used (well-hidden) radios and carrier pigeons to report German troop movements to British contacts across the English Channel. Even if the gold never made it back to France, at least the Germans wouldn't be able to use it to buy the vital imports they needed to build, maintain, and fuel their jeeps, tanks, planes, and U-boats.

On August 14, 1942, the Bells arrived by taxi at Takoradi Harbor, the oldest seaport in Gold Coast. Porters carried their luggage down the pier and up the gangplank of the *West Lashaway*. Crewmen loaded food and water, polished the rails, and cleaned the windows on the bridge. Some spoke English, others Spanish, Portuguese, Italian, or Tagalog. Ten thousand foreign-born crewmen worked on American cargo ships during World War II. They may not have been US citizens, but they all risked their lives for the war effort.

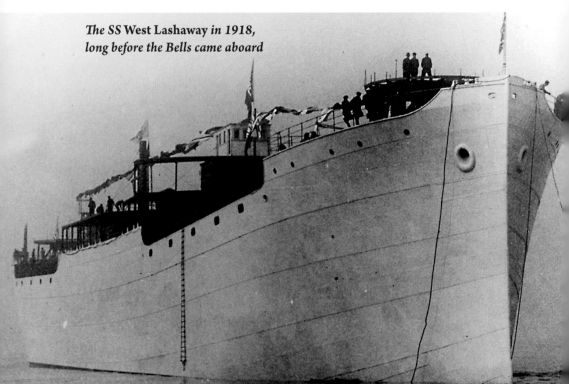

The SS West Lashaway *in 1918, long before the Bells came aboard*

Brooklyn-born Captain Bogdan was there to greet the Bells. A veteran of two decades on the high seas, he wore a white cap and a double-breasted blue uniform with four horizontal gold stripes on the sleeves: the insignia for US naval captains since 1881.

Lining the rail and waving to the Bells were eight US Navy guards. A ninth navy man, twenty-one-year-old Gunner's Mate Dalton Munn of Columbia, South Carolina, was oiling the four-inch, fifty-millimeter gun mounted on the poop deck.

Another family of fleeing Americans was also on hand to greet the Bells. The parents, Harvey and Vera Shaw, were Baptist missionaries who'd been serving in Bambari in the Central African Republic. Their three children were Richard, age thirteen; Georgia, age ten; and Carol, age seven. Twelve days earlier, the five of them had embarked from Matadi.

Captain Bogdan showed the Bells to their cabin, which Robert described as "small but comfortable." In addition to a wooden chest of drawers and a wash basin, there were two sets of bunk beds with a night table in between. Before they unpacked and stowed their luggage, Ethel, Mary, and Robert held hands, thanked God for providing this ship for their return voyage, and prayed for a safe trip.

The next day the *West Lashaway* sailed. "When we left Takoradi," wrote Mrs. Bell, "the sun shone brightly, and the south wind blew softly. It was an ideal time to voyage across the South Atlantic." The trip, she said, would be one of needed rest, recuperation, "and the joy of anticipated reunion with friends and loved ones."

Four thousand and eighty miles west was the British colony of Trinidad (now Trinidad and Tobago). In 1942, this southernmost island in the Caribbean was home to a recently built air and naval facility shared by the British and Americans. Captain Bogdan was scheduled to arrive in Trinidad on September 2. From there he would pilot the ship north to New York Harbor and then on to his final destination of Fall River, Massachusetts.

The *West Lashaway* sailed south of Ivory Coast and west of Liberia and Sierra Leone. The last signs of civilization were twinkling lights from Sierra Leone's capital of Freetown. After that, the only twinkling came from heavenly bodies in the night sky.

During the first week, the weather was ideal: blue skies, warm breezes, gentle ocean swells. Being both civilians and missionaries, the Bells and Shaws received special treatment on the ship. At mealtimes Captain Bogdan invited both families to join him "in his handsomely appointed dining room."

Robert, Mary, and the Shaw children quickly made friends with the crew, and "there was no spot on the ship in which they were not welcome." One pleasant surprise was a menagerie of animals and birds that crewmen had brought aboard with the hope of selling them in the United States. The baboon and the African crowned cranes were kept in wooden cages, but two chimpanzees and several spider monkeys cavorted around the ship as they pleased. Robert liked to chase the chimps, but after the female bit him on the leg, he learned to keep his distance. Likewise, the messboys learned to veer away from the birdcages after one of the crowned cranes stuck its head through the bars and pecked at a tray of charred steaks being carried to the dinner table.

Mrs. Bell recalled many hours sitting in a deck chair, reading, or standing at the rail watching flying fish and rollicking dolphins, sightings that brought to her mind words from Psalm 107: "They that go down to the sea in ships, that do business in great waters; these see the works of the Lord and his wonders in the deep." In those moments it sometimes could seem as if the war was far away. But every day it moved closer. "We knew of course that we should have to pass through the danger zone," she wrote, "and we had heard many stories of good ships that had fallen prey to U-boats whose captains called the South Atlantic their 'happy hunting grounds.'"

Captain Bogdan, too, was painfully aware of recent history. He knew that in mid-January that year, just five weeks after Germany had declared war on the United States, U-boats had arrived in American waters and begun sinking ships near New York Harbor; the Jersey Shore; Virginia Beach; Cape Hatteras, North Carolina; and Jacksonville, Florida. Nearly every day, the *New York Times* told of another sinking, and many articles were accompanied by gruesome pictures of burned and bandaged survivors.

In coastal towns, you didn't need to read about it. You could stand on the shore and see black smoke, or you could walk along the beach and find ropes and ship timbers and soggy boots and black clots of oil. By the time Captain Bogdan left New York in early April, the United States had lost more than a hundred cargo ships and oil tankers, most carrying vital war material to England, North Africa, and America's new ally, Russia. For more than four months, the Eastern Sea Frontier was "the most dangerous area for merchant shipping in the entire world."

Where was the US Navy? Why no protection for coastal shipping lanes? Why were the lights along the East Coast not turned off at night? Good questions.

According to historian Michael Gannon, the person in charge was Atlantic Fleet Commander Ernest J. King. He was the one

NO ORE FOR HITLER'S WAR

France wasn't the only country to deprive the Nazis of gold. Norway shipped fifty tons of the precious metal to the United States and Canada; Poland sent eighty-one tons on a years-long odyssey through five countries before it, too, ended up in New York and Ottawa; and Britain sent a mind-boggling 1,500 tons (worth $160 billion in today's dollars) to Canada.

U-boats sinking ships during the war was common and problematic, and many newspapers reported deaths

individual, wrote Gannon, who "must be assigned the final responsibility for the US Navy's failure to prevent America's worst-ever defeat at sea." Gannon noted that by failing to act in a timely and decisive way, King was "like a sentry asleep at his post." Another historian, Ladislas Farago, wrote that "the Navy's failure . . . to fight the U-boat," and to "imbue the fight with the spirit of the hunter, was in the final analysis, one of the causes for our defeat at this stage." King would later claim that once the war began, his primary focus was stopping Japan in the Pacific, and that he lacked the tools (ships, sailors, and aircraft) to protect coastal traffic from Maine to Florida. He also maintained that merchants and restaurant owners would never accept an evening blackout. So King never ordered one, and U-boat captains continued to sink ships silhouetted by the glow from coastal towns and cities.

Finally after sixty days of "tragically unnecessary blood and brine," and after being "inundated with complaints and advice from all quarters," including the White House, King assigned nine destroyers to East Coast shipping lanes, and he ordered all cargo ships to travel in protected convoys. These defensive measures dramatically lowered the number of sinkings and forced U-boat captains to move southward into the target-rich Caribbean Sea. Every ship carrying Brazilian coffee, Bolivian bauxite, Mexican chocolate, or Texas oil to the East Coast of the United States passed through that body of water. And like the *West Lashaway*, those ships traveled solo.

Starting on the fifth day of their voyage, Captain Bodgan scheduled a daily evacuation drill. This was "not the slipshod affair it so often is on round-the-world liners," wrote Mrs. Bell, "but a duty that was religiously gone through, and which we had to perform expeditiously and efficiently, as something on which our lives might well depend." Robert recalled Bodgan telling everyone "to prepare for any possible emergency by placing all valuables in a ditty bag to be kept readily at hand in one's own quarters." Mary wrote, "We had numerous drills and knew well which lifeboat was ours."

At night the entire ship was blacked out. Thick curtains covered portholes, hallways, and any cracks that might show light. Smoking was prohibited on deck lest the glowing ash alert the enemy. The curtains made it stuffy and hot in the Bells' cabin, so Mary asked if she and Robert could take their blankets and pillows and sleep out on the deck. Mrs. Bell gave the okay. "This was so much fun," wrote Mary. "We planned to sleep there every night until we arrived in New York City."

I SEE U!

In 1941, with war spreading across Europe and Asia, the United States Navy took control of the US Coast Guard. The navy retained the newest ships and left the coast guard with seventeen old gunboats, most of which were assigned to escort duty on North Atlantic convoys. After devastating losses along the Atlantic seaboard, a New York yacht club offered the Navy thirty boats with "experienced skippers and skeleton crews." These pleasure craft couldn't battle U-boats, but crewmen could report sightings and locations. At first, Navy Admiral Ernest King scoffed at the idea, but after criticism, he accepted the offer. The coast guard organized this volunteer force and dubbed it the Corsair Fleet. Others called it the Hooligan Navy. How effective was it? Not very. In one instance, a U-boat surfaced directly underneath a yacht and lifted it two feet in the air. Another time a U-boat surfaced alongside a yacht. The U-boat commander shouted in perfect English, "Get the hell out of here, you guys! Do you want to get hurt? Now scram!"

It wasn't until the late afternoon of August 25, ten days into their journey, that the first bit of inclement weather blew in. Robert headed below deck to play cards with the navy guys who had taught him poker.

Up on the bridge, Captain Bogdan watched the skies darken. Over the next hour rain fell, thunder boomed, and lightning flashed. Looking at the instrument panel, Bogdan saw the magnetic needle on the ship's big compass gyrate wildly. There it was! The same kind of electromagnetic variation Professor Oersted had observed and documented in Copenhagen more than a century earlier.

One of the scientists who read Oersted's report lived in London. After re-creating the experiment and witnessing the compass needle's flip from vertical to horizontal, this young man started jotting down some thoughts. His name was Michael Faraday, and as one biographer put it, "It's impossible to imagine a world without his contributions to science."

A painting of Michael Faraday from 1842, overlaid with a drawing of his electromagnetic rotation experiment

CHAPTER 5
MAKING THE CONNECTION

Fig 3.

MICHAEL FARADAY came into the world on September 22, 1791. He was the third of four children born to a blacksmith and a farmer's daughter. The six Faradays lived in "cramped quarters over a stable" in central London. When Papa James Faraday became sick and unable to work, his wife, Margaret, gave each of her children a loaf of bread and told them it had to last for a week.

Michael was thirteen when his schoolmistress mocked him because he couldn't correct a speech disorder. *Rs* were the problem, and with the surname Faraday and an older brother named Robert, the letter was unavoidable. The schoolmistress went so far as to give Robert a halfpenny to buy a cane so that he might thrash the issue out of young Michael. Robert would have none of it. He ran home to tell his mother, who promptly pulled both boys out of school.

Michael went to work as a delivery boy for a bookshop. He was hardworking and reliable, and after a year the shop's owner, Mr. George Riebau, promoted Faraday to apprentice bookbinder. At the time there was no machine to compress loose pages of a book. Instead a bookbinder had to pound them together with a heavy, short-handled hammer. Faraday told a friend that he was soon able to "strike 1000 blows in succession without resting—a feat requiring . . . a large amount of muscular strength & considerable practice."

As Faraday's biceps expanded, so did his range of knowledge. Mr. Riebau allowed him to read the books he bound, including the latest edition of *Encyclopedia Britannica*, first published in 1768. Faraday wrote that he "delighted in . . . the electrical treatises" in the encyclopedia, and with Riebau's permission he began staying after work to conduct "simple experiments" using whatever materials he could snag for a few pennies at secondhand shops. His improvised lab was soon cluttered with voltaic piles; "copper and zinc electrodes; coils of wire; bottled acids; [and] glass cylinders for generating and storing electricity."

Word of this self-taught scientist got around, and shortly after turning twenty-one, Faraday received and accepted a job offer from London's premier scientific establishment, the Royal Institution. For twenty-five shillings a week, he would sweep the halls, light the fireplaces, maintain the equipment, and wash out the beakers and bottles. The position included lodging in the attic along with "as many coals and candles that he wanted." Faraday also asked for some laboratory aprons and "permission to use the apparatus for his own experiments." Permission was granted. A friend commented, "No one even at this early stage of [Faraday's] career could avoid noticing his great dexterity in using Apparatus & in constructing, for temporary use, any thing that he happened to require."

At the age of twenty-four, Faraday published his first scientific paper on the chemical secrets of limestone. At the time he said, "My fear was greater than my confidence, and both far greater than my knowledge." But seeing his words in print, he said, "increased my boldness," and over the next three years, Faraday got bold enough to publish thirty-six more papers on subjects ranging from static electricity to chemical reactions to coal mine ventilation.

In the summer of 1821, Faraday married twenty-year-old Sarah Bernard. The Royal Institution gave the newlyweds a three-room apartment on the second floor. Faraday loved that his lab was mere steps from his front door so he could conduct experiments at all hours. That same summer, the editor of a scientific journal asked Faraday to write an article about Oersted and the latest developments in electromagnetism.

Faraday spent July and most of August reading articles on the subject. On one of his customary afternoon walks, he considered what might happen if he dangled an electrified wire next to an unmovable magnet. Would the collision of electric and magnetic forces cause the wire to move? He suspected it would. But what kind of movement, exactly? Would the wire mimic a carousel and whirl around its longitudinal axis? Or would the collision of forces cause the wire to orbit around the magnet "like a tiny satellite"? Faraday predicted it would orbit. But testing his hypothesis required a device that could loosen the grip of gravity. This is where a tinkerer like Faraday had an advantage over professors. They could build mathematical models, but Faraday could build *real* ones.

One day in September 1821, Faraday descended to the basement laboratory. Tagging along to watch was fourteen-year-old George Bernard, his wife's brother.

Faraday dumped a ladleful of hot wax into a bowl, and while the wax was still liquefied, he squished an iron bar magnet into it. Once the wax hardened and held the magnet in place, Faraday poured in some mercury, a silvery-white chemical element he chose for two reasons. One, mercury is the only common metal that is liquid at room temperature, and two, it conducts electricity. The mercury covered everything but the top half inch of the magnet. It looked like a bowl of mushroom soup with a crouton floating on top.

Next to the bowl, Faraday placed a two-foot tower that he cobbled together from scraps of metal. The tower resembled an upside-down *L* with the short leg reaching over the bowl. From the tip of that leg, Faraday hung a wire long enough so the bottom inch or two dipped into the mercury. Next to the tower he plunked a voltaic pile—a battery. From one end of the battery, he ran a wire to the top of the *L*. From the other end he ran a wire into the mercury. Now there were three wires, and together with the mercury they created an unimpeded path—a circuit—for continuous electrical flow. And even if the dangling wire began moving through the "mushroom soup," the circuit would remain unbroken, because electricity flows through mercury.

Young George watched expectantly as his brother-in-law turned on the battery's power. The current traveled through the wires. When the magnetic force *generated* by the live wires met the magnetic force *surrounding* the magnet, the dangling wire did indeed begin moving through the mercury, rotating *around* the magnet.

"We have succeeded!" shouted Faraday. He and George mimicked the rotating wire and danced around the table—once, twice, three times!

Michael Faraday was the first person to convert electrical energy into continuous mechanical motion. In other words, he invented the electric motor. He and George celebrated by going to the circus.

Three years after this thrilling breakthrough, Faraday was named director of the Royal Institution's laboratory at a salary of one hundred British pounds a year (about fourteen thousand pounds today). The thirty-three-year-old science whiz now had to curtail his original research and spend much time and talent on what he called "common place employment." This included overseeing building maintenance, supervising porters and servants, purchasing equipment (including seat cushions), dispensing scientific advice to politicians, and trying to figure out a method for slowing the corrosion of the copper hulls on British warships.

More to Faraday's liking were the public lectures he gave at the Royal Institution. Topics included electricity, combustion, common metals, and the chemical history of the candle. Sound dull? Think again. This was dazzling Friday-night entertainment with Faraday as "showman, shaman, and storyteller." Audience members young and old would whoop with amazement as Faraday made his hair stand on end, wrote on paper with an electric pen, repelled soap bubbles with a magnet, or ignited a gas jet with a spark from his finger. "Always remember," Faraday told his audience, "that when a result happens, especially if it be new, you should say, 'What is the cause? Why does it occur?' and you will in the course of time find the reason." Talking about water and ice, he said, "You know very well that ice floats upon water; . . . Why does the ice float? Think of that and philosophize."

In 1831 Faraday turned forty. He could feel Father Time breathing down his neck, and yet he still had a long to-do list. He asked for and was granted relief from his "common place employment" so he could return to his beloved lab and continue to probe the mysteries of electricity and magnetism.

At the time there were two ways to generate electricity: by friction (such as rubbing a glass rod with a silk cloth) or by the chemical action of a battery. Each method presented problems:

ENGLAND'S EDISON

One day in 1824, Faraday cut out two round pieces of sticky rubber. To reduce the stickiness, he coated the insides with flour, leaving the perimeters flour-free. As he pressed the edges together, Faraday left a tiny opening through which he injected hydrogen, which is fourteen times lighter than air. Then he sealed up the hole and watched the world's first toy balloon rise to the ceiling of his lab. Toy manufacturers began making rubber balloons the following year.

Faraday's electric motor was also developed quickly. In 1839, an electric boat made its debut on the Neva River in Saint Petersburg, Russia. It carried fourteen passengers and traveled three miles per hour. Faraday's dynamo become widespread in the 1880s, "when the introduction of electric lights and electric trains created a demand for huge amounts of electricity and a distribution system to keep them going."

frictional electricity was difficult to measure and control, and batteries were "expensive, noxious, and hard to maintain." Could there be a third way?

Every scientist knew by then that a magnetic halo forms around an electrified wire. Faraday reasoned that if electricity generates magnetism, perhaps the converse was true: magnets can generate electricity. Other scientists were pondering that possibility as well. Many had already tried to coax electricity from various arrangements of magnets. None had succeeded.

Earlier that summer, Faraday had asked a lab assistant (and former soldier with the Royal Artillery) to cast an iron ring six inches in diameter and almost an inch thick. Around each half of the ring, Faraday coiled a copper wire, and around every swirl of copper coil he painstakingly wrapped twine. Finally, he covered each half of the iron ring with a separate calico cloth. Why all the swaddling with twine and cloth? Because Faraday wanted to make sure there was no metallic contact between one coil and another, or between one half of the ring, A, and the other half, B. If there

Michael Faraday lectures at the Royal Institution in London

were to be any electric or magnetic "communication" between A and B, he wanted to be certain it was wireless.

Faraday connected A to a battery. He knew that when he turned on the power, an electric current would spiral through the copper coils around A, transforming that half of the iron ring into an electromagnet. He also knew that the magnetic halo over A would drift over to B. The question he wanted to answer: Does that magnetic halo carry an electric force? If it did, then he should be able to detect an electric current swirling around B. When designing this experiment, Faraday made sure to extend the wire ends of the B coil so they bent away from the iron ring and passed over a "delicately balanced, horizontal, magnetized needle." Any quiver of that needle would indicate the presence of electricity in B.

Faraday fed electric current to A. The needle quivered. But just once. Electric current continued to flow into A, but the needle didn't move after one initial twitch. When Faraday cut the power to A, the needle quivered, again only once. That might have been why other scientists had missed the effect. You had to be staring at the needle to notice that it moved only when power was switched on or off. Faraday said it seemed "as though a wave of electrical power had surged through [B], and almost immediately subsided."

Faraday never explained how he happened to look at the needle at just the right moment. Perhaps he had a hunch. Maybe he got lucky. Whatever the case, he proved that a magnetic force generates its own electrical force, and that both forces braid themselves together and move invisibly through space.

One more experiment remained. Yes, Faraday had generated electricity from magnetism, but only after supplying the initial jolt of battery power to A. Could he achieve a similar result without a battery? Could he generate an electric current using only magnets?

Faraday spent a morning and most of an afternoon placing a coil-wrapped iron cylinder among various configurations of magnets. The cylinder was wired to a galvanometer to register any hint of electricity. After each new arrangement, Faraday glanced at the galvanometer. Nothing. Toward the end of the day, he "tied together the ends of two bar magnets to form a hinged, V-shaped 'jaw'" and placed the cylinder inside. Picture an open-mouthed alligator about to chomp down on a vertical celery stalk.

From the ring experiment, Faraday had picked up a vital clue: The compass needle twitched only when the electric current surged or subsided. In other words, only when there was a variation in the flow of electricity. Could the same principle apply to magnetism? And if so, how to vary the amount of magnetic force acting on a coil-wrapped iron cylinder? Don't overthink it: the simple answer is the right one. To vary magnetic force, you *move the magnet*! That's what Faraday did. He widened and narrowed the magnetic jaw—once, twice, three times. Each time, the needle on galvanometer twitched. All it took to convert magnetism into electricity, he wrote, was "a mere momentary push or pull" of the top magnet. If Faraday had been able to swap the galvanometer with a modern-day lightbulb, the movement of the magnet over the cylinder would have lit up the bulb. In his diary Faraday noted his "distinct conversion of Magnetism into Electricity." He had, in effect, invented the dynamo—a machine that converts mechanical energy into electrical energy. Dynamos would later be called generators.

Being the first person to tiptoe into this unexplored and invisible scientific territory, Faraday had to invent a vocabulary to explain his findings. He chose the word *field* to describe the space around a magnet or a live wire. These magnetic and electrical fields, he said, send out "invisible strings," which he called "lines of force." And along those lines travel waves of energy that resemble waves "upon the surface of disturbed water." It's these waves—these vibrations of the lines of force—that send electromagnetic energy rippling or radiating outward through space. Faraday called the electromagnetic waves "ray-vibrations," and he began to suspect a relationship between ray-vibrations and light. Imagine that in 1846—when factories ran on waterpower, darkened streets were lit with whale-oil lamps, and people traveled by horse and buggy. Wow!

When anyone asked Faraday for a practical demonstration of his theory, he put an iron nail and a magnet on separate ends of a table and then explained that the seemingly empty space between the two objects was not, in fact, empty. Rather, that space or "field" was crisscrossed by a web of both magnetic and electric lines of force, and it was the magnetic force lines that pulled the nail toward the magnet.

One question was always: But how? Does the magnet shoot its magnetic force toward the nail? The answer was no. Magnetism was not the result of an action and reaction. Magnetism resulted from the nail encountering the magnetic lines of attraction and repulsion that have always extended over the whole of nature. This

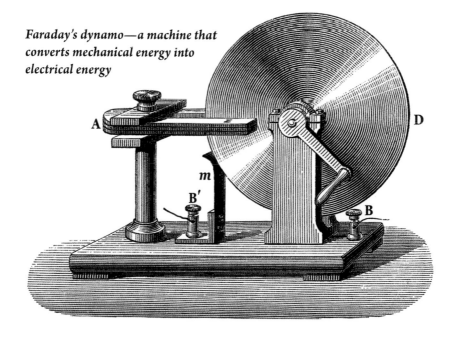

Faraday's dynamo—a machine that converts mechanical energy into electrical energy

is similar to how the pull of gravity has *always* extended over the whole of nature. In his writings, Faraday urged readers to focus less on material objects, such as magnets and electric circuits, and more on the space surrounding those objects. It's there, he wrote, in that field, that one can observe the "tugs and nudges of force."

When Faraday presented his ideas to a Royal Institution crowd of university-educated scientists, a friend called it "one of the most singular speculations that ever emanated from a scientific mind." Others in the audience were not so complimentary. Many were bewildered. When someone later asked Faraday to define "lines of force," he admitted he couldn't. "I merely threw out as matter for speculation, the vague impressions of my mind," he wrote. Okay, so if he couldn't define his terms, perhaps he could translate "lines of force" and "ray-vibrations" into some sort of mathematic language so others could see his calculations and design their own experiments. No, turns out he couldn't do that either. This son of a poor blacksmith knew his times tables and a little geometry, but that was about it. In Faraday's lab notebooks, there was not one mathematical symbol.

This was a problem because the language of science (and of nature) is not words—it's triangles, circles, equations, and the like. That's been the case ever since the sixth century BCE when famous Greek mathematicians (such as Pythagoras, Archimedes, and Euclid) starting writing down formulas and properties. Galileo, the father of physics, wrote in 1623 that trying to explain the universe without mathematical language is like "wandering in a dark labyrinth." English mathematician Sir Isaac Newton, born the year Galileo died, wrote that "God created everything by number, weight, and measure." Ricardo Nirenberg, a present-day mathematician, wrote that numbers allow us "to build stable bridges between our minds and the world."

Faraday was unable to build such a bridge. "I confess my feeling of great insufficiency in these matters," he wrote. "It is a matter of serious regret to me that I am no mathematician; if I could live my life over again, I would study mathematics; it is a great mistake not to do so, but it is too late now."

Despite this "great insufficiency," despite his poor reception at the Royal Institution, and despite being warned in a popular London journal to stay "off the ground on which he cannot walk," Faraday kept "working away at magnetism." All the while he remained unafraid "of appearing ridiculous or ignorant before the world of science."

Ironically it may have been Faraday's meager math skills that led to his wide-ranging discoveries. His lack of schooling impelled him to be a hands-on scientist. Instead of writing and rewriting long equations, Faraday devised thousands of experiments and then felt his way by intuition, and as he put it, "by facts placed closely together." He wrote to a colleague, "Experiments are beautiful things, and I quite revel in the making of them. Besides they give one such great confidence and, as I suspect that a good many think me somewhat heretical in magnetics or perhaps rather fantastical, I am very glad to have them to fall back upon."

FIELD OF BEAMS

Faraday's field theory contradicted the ideas of the great seventeenth-century English scientist and mathematician Isaac Newton. Newton had acknowledged that there could indeed be interaction between two objects even if they weren't touching each other. He called this "action at a distance." The moon pulls on the earth even though it is "at a distance." An iron nail is pulled by a magnet that's "at a distance." Okay, but how did Newton explain that pull? Answer: He couldn't. Late in life he concluded that God must have something to do with it. Newton's followers left God out of it, but they still had no idea how electric, magnetic, and gravitational impulses were conveyed through the emptiness of space. Faraday was the first person to posit that those empty "fields" were not so empty after all.

Continuing experimentation became difficult after Faraday began experiencing headaches, memory lapses, double vision, and muscle cramps. At times his writing hand became so gnarled, and as he put it, "disobedient to the will," that he couldn't form a single letter. Other times he felt "giddiness and confusion" in his head, and his memory was "so treacherous" he couldn't "remember the beginning of a sentence to the end." These afflictions may have resulted from stress and overwork. Or maybe they were caused by all the chemical gases he inhaled during thousands of lab experiments. There were times when his doctors forbade him "the privilege and pleasure of working or thinking" and sent him to the country for months of rest and recuperation.

Despite these chronic problems, Faraday refused to retire. Once his mind reset itself and his fingers unfurled and his daytime sleepiness subsided, he got on the London train and returned to the Royal Institution to continue his work. Always alone. His "intensely personal style of working" could not be taught or imitated. Neither could his drive, his genius, or his delight in acquiring knowledge for its own sake. "I have seen many who would have been good and successful pursuers of science," he wrote, but "it was the name and the reward they were always looking forward to— the reward of the world's praise. In such there is always a shade of envy or regret over their minds, and I cannot imagine a man making discoveries in science under these feelings."

It would be nice to report that Faraday's colleagues finally saw the light, and that the former bookbinder received the acclaim he so richly deserved. That didn't happen. Faraday couldn't understand why his fellow scientists continued to "rest content with darkness" and to cling to old ideas that hang "as dead weights upon our thoughts." Faraday lamented to his niece, "How few understand the physical lines of force! They will not see them, yet all researches on the subject tend to confirm the views I put forth."

To a colleague he wondered, "Where would our knowledge of . . . the voltaic current have been under such a restraint of the mind?"

In his final years of work at the Royal Institution, Faraday again turned his attention to public matters, such as cleaning up the sewage in the River Thames, removing dirt from paintings and sculptures in London's museums, brightening illumination from lighthouses, and improving science education in the public schools. At the time it seemed as if his electromagnetic theories might be at worst consigned to the dustbin of history or at best "left as an inheritance to future ages."

Then came a mail delivery on a chilly February afternoon in 1857. Stuffed in among letters, pamphlets, and scientific journals was a big white envelope. The sender was someone named J. Clerk Maxwell. Faraday didn't recognize the name. The return address was 129 Union Street in Aberdeen, Scotland. That didn't ring a bell either. Despite his gnarled fingers and trembling hand, Faraday managed to tear open the envelope.

It was a similar unexpected communication that created intrigue on the bridge of the *West Lashaway* on the last Saturday in August 1942. A wireless message had arrived in the ship's cramped and windowless radio hut. After decoding it, the radio man, Harold "Sparks" Van Cott, took it up to Captain Bogdan in the control room. The captain read it, grimaced, looked up, and read it again. He would have to make a decision. Quickly.

CHAPTER 6
TIN FISH

THE RADIO MESSAGE ordered Captain Bogdan to alter his ship's course. Instead of continuing east toward Trinidad, he was to turn northward and aim for Saint Thomas in the British Virgin Islands. No explanation. Was the message real or phony? Was it intended to steer him away from a pack of U-boats or drive him into the middle of danger? Captain Bogdan had good reason to be suspicious. He and his fellow ship captains knew that since the start of the war, German agents had been sending deceptive radio messages from secret South American hideouts. In April 1942, General George C. Marshall, the United States Army chief of staff, said that German spies in Brazil posed a "deadly peril" for Allied ships and planes in the South Atlantic. What Bogdan didn't know was that within the last few weeks, "two or possibly three" U-boats had blown up seven ships in Brazilian waters and sunk two more "close to Trinidad."

Bogdan would have liked to send a radio message to Trinidad asking for verification of the course correction, but that was too risky. It would reveal his position to anyone monitoring radio traffic, including enemy U-boats.

In wartime, the fate of a fighting unit or a ship or even a nation can sometimes be sealed by one person making one decision based on the available information at the time. All Bogdan had to go on was prior knowledge, experience, and the paper in his hand. He chose to ignore the message and stay the course.

The next day the *West Lashaway* was about four hundred miles east of Trinidad and moving at ten miles per hour. "The day was beautiful," wrote Mrs. Bell, "the sun rising that morning in unclouded splendor to chase away the darkness of the night."

After Mrs. Bell led a morning worship service, the Bell and Shaw families joined Captain Bogdan for a "sumptuous noonday dinner" of corned beef and ship's biscuits, capped off by, wrote Robert, a "memorable slice of pumpkin pie." After taking his last bite, Robert asked to be excused.

"Permission granted," said Bogdan with a smile. Robert headed below deck to hang out with his navy pals and join their never-ending poker game. Mary and the Shaw children were also excused. They went out on deck to watch for porpoises and the flying fish that "darted like streaks of silver from the sea."

After lingering over a second cup of tea, Mrs. Bell took her book out on deck. She read for a half hour before returning to her cabin, where she kicked off her shoes, slipped out of her dress, and lay down for a nap. She noted that Mr. and Mrs. Shaw "were also resting in their cabin."

It was 2:31 in the afternoon when one of the lookouts shouted, "Torpedo wake, starboard amidships!" Alarms shrieked. Seconds later, the lookout screamed, "Second torpedo! O my God."

FOLLOW THAT OINK!

Crewmen's accounts of trading vessels sailing among the Caribbean Islands in the early 1900s often mention a pig on board. If a captain got lost or couldn't see through fog or darkness, the pig was tossed overboard. Pigs have excellent swimming and navigational skills, and they led boats toward the nearest land. Some of these porcine water guides ended up on U-boats after vessels were torpedoed. In fact, three little pigs were picked up by U-162. The first two made good dinners for the

These underwater missiles (or "tin fish," as Mrs. Bell called them) were twenty-three feet long, twenty-one inches in diameter, and weighed a ton and a half. The warheads were packed with eleven hundred pounds of torpex (short for torpedo explosive), a nasty concoction of cyclonite, TNT, and aluminum flakes. Each had a motor, a propeller, a rudder, an interior guidance system, and enough battery power to travel more than three miles at a speed of thirty-five miles per hour.

Captain Bogdan ordered a hard turn, hoping to dodge one or both torpedoes. Too late. The first torpedo "hit the ship directly under me," wrote Mary, "and I was thrown to the deck." So were the Shaw children. Richard Shaw remembered "big chunks of iron flying everywhere." Carol Shaw said that after she stood up, she was able to take only a couple steps before she slipped in a puddle of palm oil, fell, and "broke [her] right elbow." Below deck Robert tossed his cards aside and raced for the ladder. In her cabin Mrs. Bell put on her dress and shoes "in one act." Robert and Mary reached the Bells' cabin just as the second torpedo hit the fuel bunkers and blew up the boilers. A spume of scalding water shot fifty feet into the air. In the Bells' cabin, the lights went dark; the wash basin fell; the bunks collapsed; and the floor began to creak, crunch, and slide out from under them.

All three of the Bells had their life vests on in a matter of seconds. Mrs. Bell led her children up a tottering ladder as the ship listed to port. Mary heard dishes breaking in the dining room.

crew. The third was a black cutie the German sailors kept as a pet. U-162's captain, Jürgen Wattenberg, named that pig Douglas since it came from the Florence M. Douglas. When U-162 returned to its base in Lorient, France, Wattenberg formally presented Douglas to the commander of the second U-boat flotilla. After that point, the little fellow's trail goes cold, but it's nice to think that Douglas might have survived the war.

They'd forgotten their ditty bags, but there was no going back. On deck the air was thick with steam and smoke. "We could hardly see," wrote Mary. They weaved their way through scattered sailors and crewmen. The Bells knew where to go, but when they arrived at their assigned lifeboat, they found only broken boards. A sailor pointed them to the other side of the deck. The Bells wobbled across the belly of the boat, grabbing shattered railings and one another. Mary and Robert jumped into the lifeboat and were helping their mom climb in when the ship suddenly shuddered and rolled to the right. Crewmen tumbled to the deck. So severe was the slope of the ship that the Bells' lifeboat jammed against the rope-and-pulley devices (called davits) that raised and lowered the boats. An officer shouted, "Get out! For God's sake, get out!"

"As I was climbing out of the lifeboat," wrote Mary, "I saw water about three inches from my foot. The next thing we knew, we were going down with the ship." The *West Lashaway* "sank beneath our feet," wrote Mrs. Bell. "We saw the blue-green sea come up to meet us," and then "the waves closed over my head."

Everyone and everything were sucked into a foaming vortex: metal beams, bed frames, tables, chairs, broken dishes, frying pans, lockers, timbers, railings, whirling propellers, bulkheads, broken drums of palm oil, bags of cacao beans, the African animals, the heavy safe full of gold, and more than fifty people. When the thunderous whirlpool ceased whirling and the watery gash closed, all that could be heard was the murmur of the waves, and all that was left on the surface was a shape-shifting oil slick and a haze of smoke. It was less than two minutes from the lookout's first warning cry to the sea swallowing the last beam of the ship.

As she was pulled downward, Mary heard the roaring suction power of the sinking ship. Figuring she had no chance to survive, she didn't struggle. "I freely let my lungs continue to function," she wrote, "only now it was water, not air, I was taking in."

Mrs. Bell expected to be dragged so deep that her life vest would be of little use. "I was sure that our last hour had come," she wrote.

Robert, too, was convinced he was going to drown.

"I shall see the children in heaven," thought Mrs. Bell.

I will "soon see Daddy and Jesus," thought Mary.

Two things prevented a heavenly reunion: cork-lined life vests and Archimedes's law of buoyancy, which says a body sinking in water is subjected to an upward force equal to the weight of the displaced water. Anyone wearing a bulgy life vest displaces more water than he or she would without the vest. So the buoyant force outweighs the sinking body and pushes it toward the surface.

Sure enough, after sinking about twenty-five feet, the three Bells leveled off and then began ascending. Up, up, up—they corkscrewed through the darkness toward the light until they burst to the surface and gulped for air. In between "coughing and gagging," Robert heard voices. He couldn't see much because palm oil coated his face. Blinking open a narrow peephole, he was able to perceive blurred shapes of the other people and objects that had also risen to the surface of the water.

Robert called out for Mary, who spluttered up salt water. Once her lungs started taking in air, she answered Robert, and he swam toward her voice. "We hugged tightly," wrote Mary, "so thankful to have each other."

"Mother!" Robert shouted. Mrs. Bell was sixty yards away and covered with so much palm oil that her kids couldn't identify her. Then she answered, "Children, over here. O thank you, Lord!"

"We swam to her," wrote Mary, "and together we held on to a plank which was part of the wreckage that littered the sea all around us."

Critically, what *wasn't* wrecked were the four wooden rafts that every cargo ship carried in addition to lifeboats. Mounted on steeply angled skids, the rafts were normally released by a loosened line. On this day no loosening was needed. The second torpedo had catapulted the thousand-pound rafts through the air and into the ocean. They were reversible, so it didn't matter which side landed up. Each raft was designed to hold about ten people.

A few crewmen had already crawled onto these rafts and freed the two oars from the storage area under the floorboard decking. They navigated through the wreckage and pulled out survivors. "Over here!" Mrs. Bell called out. "Three more over here!" As she and her children were hoisted out of the mucky water, Mrs. Bell heard one of the crewmen say, "Help me with this man, he is wounded." It was Mr. Shaw, whose cabin had fallen in on him. "Gentle hands laid him on the raft," wrote Mrs. Bell, "but he never spoke. He just lay there." Moments later, Richard Shaw was lifted onto the raft. He had not managed to get his life vest on and had survived by clinging to another man. Carol Shaw "came up in a swirl," wrote Mary, "and a sailor dove in to save her."

Suddenly a low drone could be heard over the sound of the waves. People stopped shouting, and crewmen stopped paddling. Thinking it could be a plane, they looked up. But the sound wasn't coming from the sky. It was underneath them. The water surface broke, and from the depths emerged U-66. It was big as a whale, sleek as a shark, terrifying as a sea monster, and less than fifty yards away.

The survivors heard a metallic clank as the hatch swung open. Four uniformed officers climbed out of the U-boat and up into the conning tower. Three were armed.

U-66 on August 7, 1943

Two lit cigarettes. They had a chat in German and a hearty laugh. The officer in a white cap gave an order, and the others suddenly opened fire with their automatic weapons. Shipmates still bobbing in the water ducked under the surface. People on rafts dropped onto the bottom slats. "I thought they were going to complete their evil work by killing us all," wrote Mrs. Bell. But the bullets flew high. No one was hit. The Germans, it turned out, were just testing their guns.

Captain Bogdan had heard that some U-boat captains gave survivors crackers and water and pointed them toward the nearest island or coastline. But the man in the white cap didn't address them and gave them no food, water, or geographical guidance. The Bells watched the Germans climb back down the hatch and close the cover. The U-boat's engines revved, the propellers dug in, the water bubbled, the boat eased forward, the hull sank below the surface, and the conning tower vanished. In less than half a minute it was as though the hulking gray monster had never been there.

"Anyone seen Captain Bogdan?" someone shouted.

"Right here with me."

"Who's that?"

"Bosun," said thirty-five-year-old James Peifer, who was from Pittsburgh, Pennsylvania. Bosun was short for boatswain, a naval job that dates to the founding of the US Navy in 1775. The bosun is the senior crewman of the deck and in charge of the hull, rigging, anchors, cables, and deck crew.

"Captain's hurt," Peifer said, "but he's conscious. Says we oughta bunch up."

Paddlers maneuvered the rafts into a line, crewmen tossed ropes from one raft to another, and soon the four rafts were linked up "like a cluster of canal barges." While the crewmen tied knots, a shiver of sharks appeared and circled the formation. One of these creatures was nearly twice the length of a raft. A crewman picked up an oar and jabbed the shark several times. "Best to leave him alone," said another crewman, "or else he might come back and bring his big brother."

Captain Bogdan's throat and lungs had been burned by smoke and the chemical cloud from the torpex. He was unable to stand or shout, but he was still in command. After signaling for quiet, he spoke.

"First, men, well done. Nobody could ask for more. Where's Sparks?"

"I don't think he made it," said a crewman.

Another said, "Last I seen him, he was sittin' right at his radio, but I ain't seen him since."

"That's too bad," said the captain. "I'd like to know if the poor devil had time to get off an SOS for us." Bogdan asked the crewmen on each raft to count the survivors. "I've got six, counting myself," he said. From the other three rafts came the following information.

"Nine, Captain. But one of our drums is full [of water], and we're listing."

"We've got seventeen, Captain, and we're punctured in two drums."

"Ten, Captain, but we're also taking on water."

Robert did some mental math and realized that forty-two people had survived the attack, which meant that fourteen had not.

"All right," said Bogdan, "we've got to make some changes. Our raft is undamaged. Right, bosun?"

"Aye, aye, sir."

"Then we'll take on capacity here and divide the rest among the three damaged rafts. Women and children first. Mrs. Bell? Mrs. Shaw?"

"Mrs. Shaw didn't make it, Captain," said a crewman. Neither had ten-year-old Georgia Shaw. Hearing this, Mr. Shaw "burst into sobs" and clung to his two surviving children.

"I'm sorry, Mr. Shaw," said the captain. "All right, Mrs. Bell, bring your children and the Shaw children over here."

With the sharks nosing around the column, the captain urged everyone to step carefully. Robert, Mary, and Carol Shaw followed Mrs. Bell onto the captain's raft.

"Aren't you coming with us, Daddy?" asked Carol. "I want you to come with me." Mr. Shaw didn't move. Mrs. Bell suspected the man "may have been injured much worse than we realized," unable to care for his children or to climb from one raft to another. "I'll be right here in the raft next to you," he said as he motioned for Carol to go to the captain's raft. Richard wanted to stay with his father, wrote Mrs. Bell, "but the captain would not permit it." Mr. Shaw said, "Go ahead, son." Mrs. Bell and the four children squeezed into a corner of the raft. Seeing Carol's bent and broken arm, a crewman tore his shirt and made her a sling.

The captain now had eleven on his raft including him. The three other rafts were still listing badly. "What do you think, bosun?" said the captain. "Can we take six or eight more?"

"Pretty crowded . . . with that many," replied Peifer. "Course if we let the woman and children go back to the other raft, we'd have more room for grown men."

"The woman and children are in my care, Peifer," said the captain. He reached out to Robert and drew the boy onto his big belly. "Here you go, young man," he said. "You stay right here with me."

Bogdan ordered the bosun to keep shifting people until the other three rafts rose well above the water line. After the addition and subtraction, the captain's raft had nineteen on board, packed tight as peas in a pod.

"Okay, then," said the captain, "let's check out our supplies." Though no one had retained a ditty bag, several men still had their pocketknives. The bosun and the oiler, Louis Vega (from Brooklyn, New York), jimmied open the clasp that secured supplies beneath the well. They pulled out a chest made from galvanized steel (named after you know who). The zinc-coated steel chest contained the same emergency rations found on all US Navy rafts: two sixteen-gallon kegs of drinking water, sealed tins of crackers, non-melting chocolate bars, malted milk tablets, and three hundred four-ounce cans of a protein-packed meal called pemmican, which in 1942 consisted of dried and pounded beef mixed with animal fat, sugar, raisins, and dried cranberries. In addition to the food and water, there was a first aid kit, two flares, two granite drinking cups, and a canvas tarp that could be used to collect rainwater and to shield rafters from the sun. Crewmen on the other rafts reported the same amount of food, water, and supplies.

The captain said that everyone could count on four ounces of water a day, two swigs in the morning and two at night. The daily menu would be a half-tin of pemmican in the morning and the other half for dinner. Dessert would consist of one cracker, a piece of chocolate, and a malted milk tablet.

Peifer noticed something floating by. "Look, there's a dough-nut," he said. "Grab it." This was not the sort of doughnut people dunk in their coffee. It was a rectangular cork dinghy with a slatted wooden floor. Equipped with its own minipaddles, it functioned as a two-person life raft or a tiny watercraft. Peifer offered to climb into it and paddle through the wreckage to see what he could retrieve. Bogdan approved.

A crewman yelled to Peifer that he should slit open cacao-bean bags, empty out the beans, and bring back the burlap. Others agreed that the bags could make good seat cushions and could also be cut into clothing for people who had no shirts or long pants. Poking at the sharks with his paddle, Peifer made several trips, each time returning with armfuls of burlap. He also brought back plenty of rope he found floating on the surface.

On his last trip, he paddled past the crowned cranes, still very much alive and squawking in their floating wooden cages. The keys to the locks were somewhere at the bottom of the ocean. One crewman suggested keeping them for a future dinner. Robert didn't like that idea and was glad when another crewman said, "No way, man! There's not enough meat on any one of them to make it worth the noise of keeping them." Robert was hoping that after a week or so, they'd get so thin they could slip between the bars and gain their freedom. Peifer left the cranes and saw no sign of the baboon, the chimps, or the spider monkeys.

Back on the raft, Peifer had just squeezed onto his newly cushioned seat when Robert suddenly sat up and blurted, "Oh Mother, I feel so sick." He wasn't the only one. During any life-and-death struggle, the brain and body switch to survival mode. Once the shock subsides, the mind begins reliving the terror, and the digestive system expels the salt water and the slime.

"Most everyone heaved over the side," wrote Mary. Those unable to turn spewed on the next guy.

ALL-NATURAL ENERGY BAR

The word pemmican comes from the language of the Cree people, who originally lived where Manitoba, Canada, is today. During summer months, these hunter-gatherers dried lean buffalo meat, added Saskatoon berries (also called Juneberries), and covered the mixture with rendered animal fat, which hardened and protected the food so it could be taken on buffalo hunts and used as a primary food source during lean winter months. After French and British fur trappers and frontiersmen sampled pemmican, it became a highly valued commodity. The Hudson Bay Company bought tons each year. An adult can survive for months (or even years!) consuming nothing but pemmican and water. To stay alive and healthy, an average-sized person needs an average of 2,300 calories a day. Each four-ounce tin on the rafts provided only 760 calories.

Pemmican

"For heaven's sake, man!" shouted someone who got hit.

"Sorry, man. I couldn't help it."

It was the same on all four rafts: two full hours of retching followed by a splashy seawater cleanup.

"I'm going back in the doughnut," said Peifer. "That'll make more room for everybody."

"Yeah, especially you, Chief," someone replied. "Want some company?"

Peifer answered with a headshake and a sneer as he wriggled over the side of the raft and dropped into the cork dinghy.

"I don't suppose anyone feels much like eating now," said the captain. "I think we'll hold off on the rations till morning."

As the sun set, the air cooled, and the rafters felt the clamminess of whatever clothing they had on. After asking Robert to shift position, the captain crawled into the middle of the raft and lifted himself to sit atop the food chest. He cupped his hands around his mouth and said, "Mrs. Bell, men, I don't need to tell you that we need everyone's total cooperation and support. None of us has ever been in such a tight place before, I'm sure. I hope it'll be the last time for all of us. But until help comes . . . we've got to help each other."

On all four rafts, people nodded or mumbled their agreement.

"Sure, it's going to be uncomfortable," the captain said, "but no more so for you than for the person next to you. So, I ask you, *think*! Think about what's best for the whole group." He paused, grimaced, and tried to take a deep breath. "If everyone thinks on behalf of the group, then everyone will be taken care of. And, I remind you, that naval regulations still apply, and orders given will be obeyed! Now, rest easy, and get some sleep, if you can."

The captain slid to the floor and rested his back against the food chest. Robert wasn't sure where he should sit until Bogdan patted his belly and motioned that Robert should lie there. That would be the boy's bed for the night.

Mrs. Bell asked the captain if she could recite an evening prayer. Bogdan said there was "better reason than ever to say our prayers." Mrs. Bell began speaking the words of Psalm 23: "The Lord is my shepherd; I shall not want."

The three older children were well acquainted with this passage and joined in. With Richard's prompting, even Carol spoke the few phrases she knew. "He maketh me to lie down in green pastures: he leadeth me beside the still waters. He restoreth my soul . . ."

As soon as the prayer ended, Peifer shouted from the doughnut, "Get comfortable, everybody! It's gonna be quite a night."

"There was little talking," wrote Mrs. Bell. "We . . . were barely able as yet to comprehend what had taken place." The only sounds were the wind, the waves, and the rasping of wood on wood as the rafts scraped and nudged each other. A surprisingly chilly wind came up. Mary couldn't stop shivering until a kind sailor put his burly arm over her shoulder and held her close.

Mrs. Bell barely slept that first night, but she did find great comfort in gazing at the sky. "One by one the stars came forth," she wrote, "solemn eyes that looked down upon us, gleaming on our lonely pillow, 'far, far at sea.'" And sometime in the wee hours, Mrs. Bell found herself whispering the words of Psalm 139: "If I take the wings of the morning and dwell in the uttermost parts of the sea, even there shall Thy hand lead me, and thy right hand shall hold me."

So passed the long night, "the longest," wrote Mrs. Bell, "that many of us had ever experienced." When blessed dawn broke and the sky turned crimson, she and the others "searched the horizon eagerly for some sign of a ship but saw none."

That Monday morning, August 31, 1942, Captain Bogdan, the Bells, and the other survivors found themselves in the same sort of limbo that Michael Faraday had been in nearly a century earlier. Like the rafters, Faraday's fate hinged on the timely arrival of much-needed assistance.

A photo of James Clerk Maxwell as a young man, overlaid with equations

CHAPTER 7
MAXWELL'S EQUATIONS AND HERTZ'S WAVE

FROM THE BIG WHITE ENVELOPE with the February 1857 postmark, Michael Faraday pulled a research paper entitled "On Faraday's Lines of Force." The author was a twenty-six-year-old Scotsman named James Clerk Maxwell who had written the paper two years earlier while still a student at Cambridge University.

Maxwell was born the same year that Faraday invented the dynamo (1831), and his genius was apparent early on. When he was only three years old, Maxwell's mother wrote, "He has great work with doors, locks, keys, etc. and 'Show me how it doos' is never out of his mouth. He also investigates the hidden courses of streams and bell-wires . . . and he drags Papa all over to show him the holes where the wires go through." If something "moved, shone, or made a noise" Maxwell wanted to know about it, and if an answer didn't satisfy him, he'd follow up with, "But what's the *particular* go of it?"

At age fourteen, Maxwell published a paper about all the curves that can be drawn with a pencil, a few pins, and piece of string. Considered too young to present the paper, Maxwell listened to it read aloud by a staff member at the Royal Society of Edinburgh. It was also in Edinburgh that Maxwell's father took him to an exhibition of "electromagnetic machines." The brilliant young Scot was enchanted by "the wonder of forces acting in space."

By the time he sent his paper about lines of force to Faraday, Maxwell was a professor of natural philosophy (now called physics) at Marischal College in Aberdeen, Scotland. In the paper Maxwell said that not only was he convinced Faraday was right, but that he had figured out a way to express Faraday's ideas in mathematical terms. How? By adhering to the idea that all human knowledge is based on understanding the relations between two things. "A knowledge of one thing," he wrote, "leads us a long way towards a knowledge of the other."

In Faraday's case, Maxwell related unseen fields and lines of force to another branch of physics, namely the flow of fluid, which can be seen, measured, and expressed in numbers. One historian calls Maxwell's work "one of the finest examples of creative thought in the history of science." Maxwell said he was simply making the connection between two very different phenomena.

For Faraday, it was a tough slog through Maxwell's remarkably complex equations. "I was at first almost frightened when I saw the mathematical force made to bear on the subject," Faraday wrote. But he added that he was pleased to see the "subject stood it so well." Indeed it must have given Faraday a serious jolt of joy to see his much-maligned lines of force "cloaked in the armor of mathematical symbolism." In his written reply, Faraday thanked his young

24-HOUR FITNESS

As a student at Cambridge University, James Maxwell was so busy reading, writing, talking, observing, helping a sight-challenged friend, and attending lectures that he rarely had enough time to exercise during the day. So he scheduled his workouts for two o'clock in the morning, when he would sprint through the corridors and climb up and down the stairs of his dormitory. Students who were still awake or who were awakened by his footsteps made a game of it by opening their doors and pelting their sprinting classmate with boots and hairbrushes.

Aberdeen ally and said Maxwell's research paper "gives me much encouragement." In fact, Faraday was so encouraged that he included with his thank-you note his latest research paper, in which he concluded that both electric and magnetic force "must probably" travel at the same speed as light. "I wonder what you will say," wrote Faraday. "I hope however that bold as [my] thoughts may be, you may perhaps find reason to bear with them."

Maxwell not only bore with them, he proceeded to figure out a mathematical formula that revealed the speed at which an electromagnetic wave would move through space. The number he came up with was 193,088 miles per second, which is pretty darn close to the actual speed of light (which more precise calculations later clocked at 186,000 miles per second). Maxwell replied to Faraday saying, "I think we have now strong reason to believe" that light is in fact an electromagnetic wave—a ray-vibration, as Faraday called it way back in 1846.

Faraday continued to express his abiding gratitude for this "first intercommunication" with someone of Maxwell's "mode and habit of thinking," and he added that Maxwell's latest letter "will do me much good, and I shall read and meditate on it again and again."

In October 1864 Maxwell gave a lecture asserting that with eight equations (later reduced to four), he could prove the existence of electromagnetic fields. His colleagues expected that Maxwell's equations would be accompanied by mechanical models so they could visualize the "whirring clockwork": the wheels, gears, and cogs that represent electric and magnetic power moving through space. But Maxwell's conception of the electromagnetic universe could not be depicted in models or mental images. The only metaphor he could offer was that of a bell ringer who "tugs ropes that dangle through holes in the ceiling of the belfry." The bell ringer can hear the bells ringing, but he's unable to see the clapper that produces the sound.

Maxwell's lecture was greeted with the same bewilderment as Faraday's presentation eighteen years earlier. A theory with no working model was unheard of. The famous physicist William Thompson (aka Lord Kelvin) grumbled that Maxwell "had lapsed into mysticism."

Insulted or not, Maxwell was a mystic in the sense that he had attained insight into mysteries transcending ordinary human knowledge. Thompson and his fellow scientists couldn't comprehend that Maxwell had not only "predicted *electromagnetic waves*," he had opened the door "to a new and different world."

It took about ten more years for the world's greatest mathematicians and physicists to catch up with Maxwell. When he published his huge thousand-page book (or *Treatise* as he called it) on electricity and magnetism in 1873, a colleague called it "one of the most splendid monuments ever raised by the genius of a single individual."

Nearly one hundred years later, in 1970, American physicist Richard Feynman said, "From a long view of the history of the world—seen from, say, ten thousand years from now—there can be little doubt that the most significant event of the 19th century will be judged as Maxwell's discovery of the laws of electromagnetism. The American Civil War will pale into provincial insignificance in comparison with this important scientific event of the same decade."

Feynman's colleague Freeman Dyson added, "The modern view of the world that emerged from Maxwell's theory is a world with two layers." One layer contains all the real-life things we detect with our senses. For thousands of years this was the only layer we understood. Building on Faraday's discoveries, Maxwell proved that we're surrounded by a second, invisible layer, one "not directly accessible to our senses." One way to think about Maxwell's achievement is to relate it to the work of another genius, William Shakespeare. What Shakespeare did better than anyone was to take the unseen forces of love, ambition, and jealousy, and turn them into words, sentences, and rhymes. Maxwell took the unseen forces of electricity and magnetism and turned them into signs, symbols, and numbers.

One hundred and fifty years after it was published, Maxwell's *Treatise on Electricity and Magnetism* is still in print and still widely read by physics students. But there's one thing missing from it. Maxwell "gave no indication of how [electromagnetic waves] might be produced or detected in a laboratory."

Before he was able to generate a wave, the forty-eight-year-old Maxwell began suffering from heartburn. Then came the loss of the spring in his step and a reluctance to take on any new writing assignments. When the shaking of his horse-drawn carriage proved unbearable, Maxwell suspected that he was suffering from the same disease that had killed his mother: stomach cancer. He was right. Palliative care made his last days bearable, and his mind remained sharp until the end. When he died on November 5, 1879, a colleague wrote, "The spirit of Maxwell still lives with us in his imperishable writings and will speak to the next generation by the lips of those who have caught inspiration from his teachings and example."

The same year that Maxwell died, the Prussian Academy of Sciences in Berlin, Germany, announced that it would award a

YOU KANT KNOW IF YOU DON'T ASK

Maxwell thought highly of German philosopher Immanuel Kant, who said that understanding the relationship between objects was more important than understanding the objects themselves. Echoing this idea in a college essay, Maxwell wrote that "although pairs of things may differ widely from each other, the relation in the one pair may be the same as that in the other." And "a knowledge of the one thing leads us a long way toward a knowledge of the other." To put it another way, don't ask, What is that thing over there? Instead ask, How does that thing over there relate to this thing over here?

prize of one hundred ducats (fifteen thousand dollars in today's money) to the first person who could build a device that generated the sort of electromagnetic wave Maxwell had envisioned.

At the time, twenty-two-year-old Heinrich Hertz was a student at the Physical Institute of Berlin. His professors recognized a brainiac when they saw one. Hertz's mentor encouraged him to enter the Prussian Academy competition. After considering it, Hertz concluded he didn't have the scientific know-how to create a wave-generating device. He needed to do more research. That was not a problem. "When he sat with his books," his mother recalled, "nothing could disturb him or draw him away from them." When the deadline for submitting the device arrived, Hertz still wasn't ready. Neither was anyone else. The prize went unclaimed.

Others may have stopped searching for a solution, but not Hertz. "I still felt ambitious," he wrote. The lack of prize money didn't matter. In fact, his "interest in everything connected with electrical oscillations had become keener." He reread Maxwell and the works of other prominent scientists. His diary entries from May 1884 read, "Hard at Maxwellian electromagnetism in the evening" and "Nothing but electromagnetics." Hertz told his students, "It is impossible to study [Maxwell's] wonderful theory without feeling as if the mathematical equations had an independent life and intelligence of their own, as if they were wiser than ourselves."

Not until two years later, in 1886, did Hertz decide he was ready to try to produce an electromagnetic wave. The first step was to build a device that generated sparks. He began with a plank of wood twelve feet long and three inches wide. At one end of the plank he placed a hollow zinc sphere about twelve inches in diameter (slightly bigger than a basketball). Around five feet away from that zinc sphere, just before the middle of the plank, he placed a much smaller zinc sphere, about the size of a grape. He elevated the "grape" with a wire the length of a toothpick. On the other end of the plank, Hertz put a similar pair of mismatched spheres. Using rigid copper wires, he connected each large-small pair, which made them resemble barbells with different weights on the ends. The only wireless area was a tiny gap between the two grape-size spheres in the dead center of the plank.

The setup complete, Hertz connected the two rigid copper wires to a battery that he supercharged with another Faraday invention: a transformer that either raises or lowers the amount of voltage traveling to a wire or a device. Hertz used the transformer to crank up the amount of electric voltage from a measly five volts to a much more robust twenty thousand volts. (Still a tiny amount compared to, say, the three hundred million volts generated by a bolt of lightning.)

When Hertz turned on the power, electric current sizzled down the two copper wires. Remember what Oersted found: that the "electric conflict" isn't contained by the wire. In Hertz's experiment, the electric current raced over and around the two "grape" spheres and hurdled into the wireless gap in the middle of the plank. There the electric conflict from one "barbell" collided with the electric conflict from the other "barbell," creating a flash and crackle of sparks. Faraday had called sparks "the most beautiful light that man can produce by art." Maxwell had predicted that the collision of currents would not only create a beautiful light, but would also produce electromagnetic waves. Was he right? Were invisible waves rippling outward from those sparks? There was only one way to find out.

Step two. Hertz cut the power and looked around the lab until he found a three-foot-long copper wire. He bent it into a U shape. To each end of the wire, Hertz attached a small zinc sphere. This wire and spheres now resembled a set of headphones. He propped

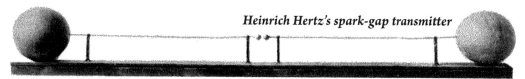

Heinrich Hertz's spark-gap transmitter

it on a table about five feet away from the long plank with the "barbells." Again Hertz sent twenty thousand volts into the wires on the plank. Again sparks crackled and snapped in the gap between the two "grapes." Then it happened. On the table five feet away from the long plank, in the gap between the two small spheres on the "headphones," Hertz saw sparks fly. That was the visual evidence he needed. *Sieh dir das an! Ich habe es getan!* (Look at that! I've done it!) Indeed he had done it. Using simple devices with no connecting wires, the twenty-nine-year-old German physicist became the first person to radiate and detect an electromagnetic wave. Close your eyes and imagine Faraday and Maxwell high-fiving.

Sad to say, Hertz had little time to build on his discovery. An infection in his jaw led to blood poisoning, and he died on New Year's Day in 1894. He was only thirty-six. One of his professors said, "In classical times one would have said that he was sacrificed to the envy of the gods."

Hertz did live long enough to deliver a notable lecture in which he advanced Faraday and Maxwell's belief that electromagnetic waves behave like beams of light. Both travel in straight lines at the same speed, and both reflect off objects in their paths.

Following that lecture, Hertz's students were eager to hear how the professor planned to use his knowledge to develop new electronic devices. But Hertz told his students he could foresee no practical use for electromagnetic waves. (Really!) His experiments were useful, he said, only because they proved that Maxwell was right. The students couldn't believe it. When pressed to consider one way he could put the waves to work, Hertz shrugged, shook his head, and said he could come up with nothing.

Okay, so the guy was a physicist rather than a visionary. It sure didn't take long, though, for other scientists to realize the gift Hertz had given them and to start building devices that transmitted electromagnetic waves. On May 13, 1897, just three years after Hertz died, a twenty-two-year-old Italian inventor living in England sent the first wireless message over open water. His name was Guglielmo Marconi, and he transmitted what was then referred to as a "Hertzian wave" from Flat Holm Island in the middle of the Bristol Channel over three miles to Lavernock Point in Wales. The technology had not yet advanced to the point where such a wave could carry words. But it could carry a message in Morse code. A technician received and decoded Marconi's message. It said, "Are you ready?"

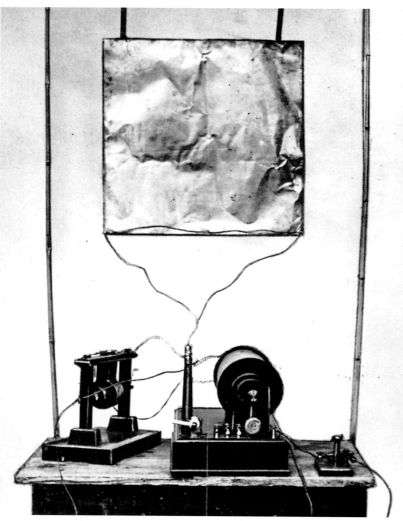

A re-creation of Guglielmo Marconi's first radio transmitter

When the enormous passenger ship the *Titanic* hit an iceberg on the night of April 14, 1912, the ship's two wireless operators used Marconi Company transmitters to send out distress signals and the global coordinates of the sinking ship. The signals were picked up by a Europe-bound passenger ship named *Carpathia*. The captain of the *Carpathia* changed course and steamed sixty miles toward the *Titanic*. By the time the *Carpathia* arrived, the *Titanic* had sunk, but crewmen were able to rescue the 706 people who had made it into lifeboats. A British government official said later, "Those who have been saved, have been saved by one man, Mr. Marconi . . . and his marvelous invention."

That same year, scientists began replacing the words *Hertzian waves* with the words *radio waves* since the waves "radiate" through

A lifeboat from the **Titanic** *approaches RMS* **Carpathia** *on April 15, 1912*

the air. Over the next several decades, radio wave technology became so advanced that by the time World War II erupted, it was possible for a U-boat in the South Atlantic to send a radio message to U-boat central command in Paris, France.

One such message arrived in Paris in the early evening of August 30, 1942. It came from U-66 and read as follows: "17:08—Smoke cloud in sight." (The military uses a twenty-four-hour time table, so 17:08 (5:08 p.m.) in Paris is 13:08 (1:08 p.m.) in the South Atlantic.) The next messages said:

"17:19—Smoke cloud out of sight;"

"18:08—Dived;"

"18:15—To Action Stations;"

"19:31—2 independent shots fired from tubes I and III. 2 hits. Heavy white detonation;"

"19:36—Surfaced;"

"19:45—Steamer sunk."

There was no mention of the four rafts or of survivors floating in the water.

CHAPTER 8
THE WAIT BEGINS

WHEN ROBERT opened his eyes after the first night on the raft, it took him a few seconds to realize where he was. Under him was the captain, whose warm belly rose and fell with each breath. When Robert looked to his right, he saw George Marano and Joe Greenwell. Marano, from White Plains, New York, was the ship's twenty-three-year-old fireman. Just before the ship's alarm had sounded, he had been working his shift in the sweltering boiler room wearing just a bathing suit. His relief man, Victor Rega, showed up a few minutes early and offered to take over. Marano thanked him and promised to "do him a good turn sometime." When asked about Rega later, Marano said, "Poor devil probably never had a chance. It could have been me, but it wasn't, that's all I know."

Forty-four-year-old Greenwell was from Pulaski, Tennessee. He was the first assistant engineer and was in the engine room when the watch officer shouted the first warning. Greenwell stayed at his post after the first hit, but the second torpedo sent a wall of seawater, palm oil, and latex pouring into the engine room. The force of the gooey mess lifted Greenwell up and shot him like a rocket through the shattered skylight. Next thing he knew, he was in the water wearing only his undershorts. When he surfaced, he found himself floating among the cocoa-bean bags. He put two under his arms, and they kept him afloat until help arrived.

Both men now wore burlap. "It's not exactly J. C. Penney's finest," Marano commented, "but it'll do."

When Robert looked left, he saw five fellows from the ship's galley, the ones who had cooked, served, and cleaned up after all the great meals. There was the second cook, Woodman Ray Potter from New York City, and the pots-and-pans guy, Levi Walker from Titus, Alabama, a one-stoplight farm town. Potter and Walker were the only two African American men on the raft. Pantryman and baker John Vargas had made the pumpkin pie Robert had enjoyed two hours before the attack. He was another New York City native. Robert McDaniel was the messman whose tray of charbroiled steaks had been nibbled by the crowned cranes. Like the captain and several others, he lived in Brooklyn. The chief cook, C. J. Rosibrosiris, sat on one of the two kegs of drinking water. Since people struggled to pronounce his name, everyone called him Rodriguez. He was from the Portuguese colony of Goa on the west coast of India, and he enjoyed pounding out a beat on the side of the keg. Behind Rodriguez were two seamen: Servior Seramos, a Filipino man with a gold tooth, and Brooklyn-born Isabelino Pacheco, whose nickname was Chico.

Peifer and Greenwell opened the keg of fresh water and filled the two granite cups. Each person took a few sips. "I can assure you," wrote Mrs. Bell, "that no water ever tasted as sweet as that." Robert said that every sip was "a precious gift."

Captain Bogdan asked the bosun to visit the three other rafts, supervise rations distribution, and advise the men on each raft to choose a leader.

While the bosun made his rounds, Robert located the little metal key attached to a tin of pemmican. He slid the key into the metal tab and turned it clockwise. *Whoosh!* The vacuum-sealed tin released a whisper of air as the metal top curled around the key. "How come we can't eat the whole tin now?" Robert asked the captain. "We've got lots of food."

"Yes, my boy," Bogdan replied, "and when we need it, the food will be there. And when we don't need it any longer, I'll see to it that you get a nice big steak instead of tinned rations. For now, you share with your sister."

Before Mrs. Bell and the children ate, they held hands and bowed their heads. Mrs. Bell said, "Our Heavenly Father, we thank Thee for the food that Thou has provided. We pray for strength to endure our difficult circumstances. We pray for courage this day . . . Amen."

The portions were small and the pemmican was rank and greasy, but everybody ate and nobody rushed. "To this day," wrote Robert later, "I eat my meals very slowly. I learned to treasure every bite." When the meal was over, the food box was tied down in the well and served as an additional seat. When Robert sat there, he saw debris from the shipwreck floating not far from the raft. He asked Joe Greenwell why it hadn't drifted farther away from the site of the sinking. Greenwell explained, "We've drifted a good long way, I'm sure. But, you see, the same current that's moving us is also moving all that junk out there. So, it's trailing alongside us."

"How fast are we drifting?" asked Rodriguez.

"Hard to say," said Marano. "Of course, without any propulsion, we fall back a little every time we move a length forward."

"Well, why not crank up some propulsion?" said Greenwell. He pointed to the oars. "We sure got enough arm power. Let's row."

"Row!"

"Are you kiddin'?"

"Hey, why not?" said Greenwell.

"Can't hurt to give it a try," said a navy man on another raft. So they did. Two men on each raft rigged up oarlocks and began rowing.

Mary thought the men's attempt at rowing was discouraging. "It took so much effort, and they made almost no headway whatever."

Greenwell concurred. "We were wasting a lot of strength we might need later on." When they decided to give up, "Nobody complained about that decision."

After a few moments George Marano said, "How about wind power?"

Peifer said, "Yea, I'll buy that," and he quickly went to work. After grabbing the two oars from his raft, Peifer asked for two from the adjacent raft. He issued instructions to Chico, Seramos, and utility man Frank Flavor, and the four of them roped one six-foot oar on top of another so that with the overlap, two oars formed a pole about eleven feet high. They did the same with two other oars. With the rocking of the raft and the lack of working space, this was no easy task, but these were longtime sailors used to improvising—and maintaining their balance—in all kinds of conditions. Peifer pulled a canvas tarp from the supply bag. The sailors unrolled it, knifed holes around the perimeter, and tied it to the oar poles.

Mrs. Bell noted that no sail-making was attempted on the other three rafts. "Most of the men there seemed to have lost heart," she wrote, "and the look of utter hopelessness on some faces was heart-rending to see." Mr. Shaw, she noted, sat for hours "with his head still in his hands. . . . The loss of his wife and Georgia seemed to have stunned him." Mrs. Bell credited Bosun Peifer for realizing that hopelessness could be fended off only by doing something. She wrote that "some action had to be taken." Indeed, Peifer made sure everyone on Bogdan's raft was active as the two masts and canvas sail were passed overhead to the eastern corners of the raft, where Peifer and his team flipped the sail vertical and lashed the bottom oars to the wooden seats. The trade winds that reliably blow east to west immediately billowed the sail and turned the lead raft into the equivalent of a "train engine" that pulled the other three rafts along.

"Good work, bosun," said the captain. "We should get quite a bit of benefit from that sail." The convoy had been under sail for thirty minutes or so when the captain summoned Greenwell. The two men had a private conversation, after which Greenwell yelled to the guys on the second raft. "Captain Bogdan wants another piece of canvas." When the canvas was passed forward, Greenwell asked Marano to help him attach it to the bottom of the sail.

"What's the idea, Greenwell?" said Peifer. "You won't get any more wind at that level."

"Captain's orders," said Greenwell.

Bogdan turned to Mrs. Bell and told her the bottom flap was a "courtesy curtain" so she, Mary, and Carol could have a bit of privacy.

"Thank you very much, Captain," said Mrs. Bell. "That's very thoughtful of you."

Yes it was, although according to Robert, there wasn't much need for privacy. After the first day's nausea and vomiting, there wasn't much food or water moving through his digestive or excretory systems. The meager daily rations must have been quickly absorbed by muscles and vital organs, because Robert didn't relieve himself—number one or number two—during the entire ordeal. Mrs. Bell said, "Throughout the experience all the men behaved towards us like gentlemen and did everything in their power to save us from embarrassment and make things as easy for us as they could." Mrs. Bell added, "With life at stake and death ever near, many of the customs and conventionalities of civilized life lose a great deal of their significance and importance."

For Peifer, sail-making was just the first activity of the day. Next he and Pacheco paddled off in the dinghy to do more scavenging in the patch of floating debris.

They returned dragging some boards, a narrow mattress, a ladder, and an armful of rope that had been used to secure cargo containers on the ship. "We'll lash these boards to the ladder and put the mattress on top," said Peifer. "Somebody can stretch out and get a little leg room from time to time." Again the sailors showed their skills as they bound the boards to the ladder in such a way that it became as sharkproof as possible. Peifer roped the floating contraption to Bogdan's raft and threw the mattress on top. Proud of his work, he said, "Why don't you give it a try, Captain? You'll be more comfortable."

The captain liked the idea. Robert slid off Bogdan's belly so the captain could crawl over the side of the raft and flop onto the mattress. He stretched out and smiled, but soon his two-hundred-plus pounds caused the bottom half of the mattress to sink below the waterline.

"Maybe it'll hold a lighter man," said the captain. "I'm coming back in." Slithering back over the side of the raft, Bogdan winced and clutched his side.

"You look like you're hurt bad, Captain," said Potter.

"It's all right, Potter. Just some burns, I guess. We mustn't make too much of them."

"Captain, you gotta take care of yourself," Potter replied. "You can't be no sofa for the kid, not if you got burns on your body." He turned to Robert and said, "Boy, you're gonna have to sit somewhere else."

"Come over here, Robert," said Mrs. Bell.

Not wanting his contraption to remain unoccupied, Peifer said, "How about putting Mrs. Bell and the kids . . . on the mattress? They're lighter than the captain. They'll float."

Greenwell didn't wait for the captain to respond. He wagged his finger at the bosun and warned him, "Lay off the lady and those kids. They don't go nowhere, you hear me?"

The bosun didn't answer. He just smirked at Greenwell, who glared back. "Already the strain of close proximity was beginning to tell on our nerves," wrote Mrs. Bell. "We had no room to move about. We could never get more than a few inches from each other. We were sure to tread on someone's feet if we shifted our position ever so little. Sharp words . . . were not infrequent." Even "the closest of friends," she said, would have a tough time in such cramped conditions.

To break the tension, the captain raised himself up and said, "Listen up, everybody. I know we're all uncomfortable with this sticky mess all over our skin and clothes, but it might be a blessing after all. We're all hoping and praying and expecting to be picked up soon, but we've got no way of telling how long we might actually be out here. In the meantime, I suggest you do your best not to scrape any of the oil off your skin. . . . it can serve to prevent some of the worst sunburn you'll ever see."

Bogdan's speech seemed to exhaust him, and he slumped back down against the supply chest with no more to say that afternoon. Nobody else said much either. "Everyone was busy with his own thoughts," wrote Mrs. Bell, "wondering, wondering."

Just before dinner, signalman Earl "Flags" Koonz started thrashing about and cackling with laughter. Ten days earlier, Flags had celebrated his twentieth birthday. Now he screamed, "When do we get off this stinkin' raft?" Some of the men tried gently to stop him from moving, and when they touched his ribs, Flags's laughter turned to cries. "Oh God, it hurts! Oh God, I wanna die!"

BLOCK THOSE RAY-VIBRATIONS

Captain Bogdan was correct that palm oil would make a good sunscreen. He may have known that the first effective "suntan lotion" had been developed four years earlier by a Swiss chemistry student named Franz Greiter, who got sunburned as he climbed Mount Piz Buin in the Alps. Before Greiter bottled and sold what he called Glacier Cream, people around the world tried all sorts of foods, flowers, and oils to protect themselves. Among them were rice, crushed jasmine petals, zinc, olive oil, sunflower oil, animal fat mixed with red ocher, paste made from the bark of the wood apple and western hemlock trees, lupine, mud, charcoal, cocoa butter, and burnt almond paste.

It wasn't just physical injuries. The explosions had jogged something in Flags's head, and he had to be warned repeatedly not to drink the salt water. "He was out of his head," wrote Mary. "He thought he was at a ball game, then he was phoning his girlfriend and later he recited part of Psalm 23." But most of the time, wrote Mrs. Bell, Flags "just sat" and "looked wistful and lonely."

As the sun lost its midday intensity and slowly dipped toward the horizon, the bosun said to the captain, "What do you think, sir? Is it time to break out the rations?"

No one had a watch, so the sun was Bogdan's timepiece. He checked the sky and agreed it was time.

"Remember, men," said Peifer, "only half a can of pemmican each. You share with the same person you ate with this morning. Two ounces of water. Measure it carefully, and don't spill any. Milk tablets, chocolate, and a cracker, same as before."

After Mrs. Bell said grace, George Marano piped up. "You know what would make this stuff more edible?" he asked.

"Nothing in the world!" answered Robert McDaniel.

"No, I'm serious," said Marano. "I know how to make these rations taste better."

"How's that, man?" wondered Levi Walker.

"We use our imagination," Marano said. "We make believe we're eating our favorite food."

Most of the other men groaned and shook their heads.

"Go 'way, Marano," said one.

"That's kid stuff," said another.

But the chief cook, Rodriguez, liked the idea and said, "I'll start the game. I'm not eating pemmican," he said as he bit into the greasy dried meat. "I'm eating biryani."

"Beer what?" asked McDaniel.

"Biryani," repeated Rodriguez, as he took another bite of pemmican. "It's a favorite dish in India and wherever Indians have traveled."

"What's it made of?"

The cook explained that biryani could be made with either chicken or lamb cut into cubes, washed in cold water, covered with spices—coriander, cinnamon, black pepper, turmeric—and mixed with ginger root, lemon juice, salt, three cloves of garlic, four large onions, and half a pint of yogurt.

"Bake it for about thirty minutes," said Rodriguez. "Then you lower the heat, say to three hundred degrees, and let it bake another half hour." By this time, several crewmen were ready to play along.

"Oooh, what an aroma!" said one. "I can just begin to catch it now!"

Another said, "Yea, it smells better than I would have expected."

"Finally," said Rodriguez, "you sprinkle . . . fried onions on top of the meat mixture, and you serve it over . . . seasoned rice."

Greenwell wanted more info on seasoned rice.

Rodriguez explained that it was rice "mixed with cardamom, cloves, cinnamon, peppercorns, salt, and bay leaves." By this time, the cook had finished his ration of pemmican. Holding out his empty tin, he said, "Anybody like some of my biryani?"

"Yessiree!"

And so began the first of many imaginary feasts. The bosun was the only one who didn't play along. "Damned stupid," he called the game. His lousy attitude didn't stop the others from pretending.

It was "a way of taking our minds off how hungry we were and how awful-tasting those rations were," said Robert. What started off as Marano's whimsy soon became a serious survival strategy. It gave people the hope and expectation that someday they'd be eating real food again. "From that hope we took strength," said Robert.

With no one hurrying through the meal, it was nearly dark before the bosun and Marano closed the supply chest and lashed it to the bottom of the raft.

Mrs. Bell and her children were halfway through their evening prayer when Flags lost it again. "It hurts too much to pray!" he shouted as he struggled to his feet and lurched toward Mrs. Bell. Before he got past the food chest, Greenwell stood up and whacked Flags across the face. The navy man moaned and dropped at Vega's and Peifer's feet. The captain felt sorry for Flags, but he had to maintain order. "Don't let him make another move like that," he said. Vega replied, "Aye, aye, captain." Flags kept whimpering, but he made no effort to stand again. Soon he got quiet.

With the ailing signalman lying at his feet, Peifer decided he needed more room. He told Seramos and Flavor to take a turn in the doughnut.

"No way," Flavor said. "I'm not spending no night in that doughnut with them sharks."

Seramos said he wasn't going to either.

"Are you disobeying my order?" said the bosun.

This awakened the captain who grunted, "Nobody gives orders but me." He told Peifer to "go to the doughnut yourself, if you care to. Otherwise, let the men be."

Everyone waited for Peifer to climb back into the doughnut. But he didn't. He stayed put. Why? Because the previous night, the sharks hadn't let him sleep. They kept thumping the doughnut with their snouts.

How did the sharks know he was in there? Peifer figured it was their acute sense of smell. That was part of it. What Peifer

ANIMAL MAGNETISM

Sharks are not the only sea creatures with built-in signal detectors. Salmon and electric eels possess magnetoreceptors that enable them to use the earth's magnetic field to guide them to their feeding and spawning grounds. That's how salmon find their way "home," and how electric eels know where to lay their eggs.

didn't know—indeed what no one knew until 1960—was that sharks have a secret weapon in their snout that allows them to detect electrical signals emitted by living creatures. What emits these signals? Muscle contractions. What if you're not moving? Do you still give off electric signals? Yes, because your heart pumps. Sharks are highly sensitive to electric fields. They can detect a heartbeat even if their prey is burrowed under sand or gravel in the sea. When a great white shark attacks, it rolls its eyes back into special sockets so they won't be scratched or bitten. In those moments a shark is blind, and it's the electric field that guides a great white to its target.

But here's the thing about a shark's built-in signal detector: In the beginning it was likely imperfect. It probably took millions of years to evolve into a finely tuned mechanism of interacting parts and processes. The same sort of evolution and fine-tuning occurred in the field of man-made signal detection—although it didn't take nearly as long.

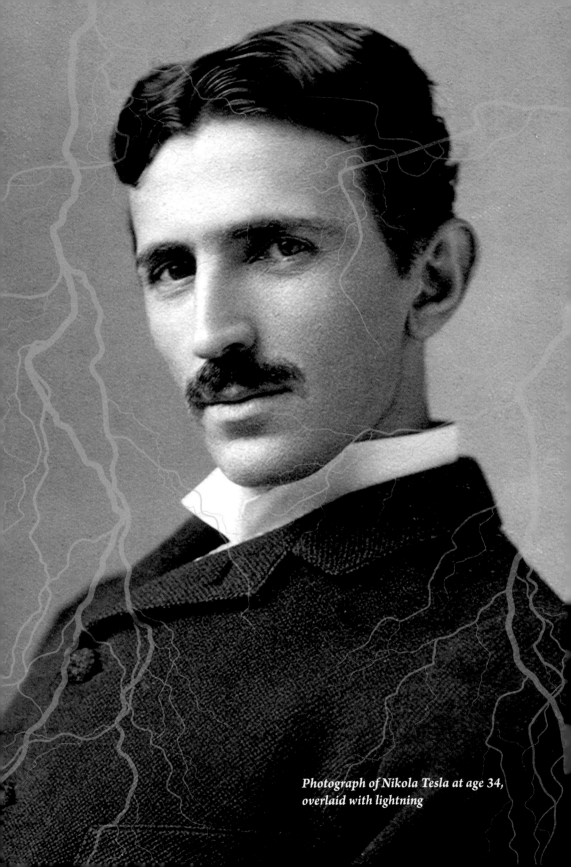

Photograph of Nikola Tesla at age 34, overlaid with lightning

CHAPTER 9
Humble Beginning

SIX YEARS AFTER Hertz's death, in 1900, a Serbian American inventor named Nikola Tesla (yes, the one the car is named after!) wrote about a connection between sound waves and radio waves. Just as a loud shout reflects off a distant wall, "so an electrical wave is reflected," wrote Tesla, and that reflection should enable us "to determine the relative position or course of a moving object such as a vessel at sea."

Like Faraday and Maxwell, Tesla was far ahead of his time, and he could never find financial backing for his idea. This didn't surprise him. "The scientific man does not aim at an immediate result," he wrote. "He does not expect that his advanced ideas will be readily taken up." Tesla compared his work to that of a farmer planting seeds for a later harvest.

The first "harvest" came four years later, when a German inventor named Christian Hülsmeyer raised enough money to build what he called a telemobiloscope. This device used Hertz's spark-gap transmitter and a receiving antenna connected to a bell. The inventor claimed the bell would ring when a reflective signal was received. At a public demonstration, Hülsmeyer transmitted a radio wave that traveled through a cloth curtain and reflected off a metal gate. The device rang out with a *ding, ding*! The success was widely reported in German newspapers, and Hülsmeyer promptly offered to sell his system to the German navy for a modest price. Maybe the price wasn't modest enough; maybe the navy engineers resented an outsider stepping on their turf; or maybe the military planners preferred to work with what they knew. Whatever the reason, German naval officers said they weren't interested. Hülsmeyer then offered his device to the Dutch navy and got another rejection.

Twelve years later, in 1916, two electrical engineers gave the German navy a second chance to say *ja*. In the middle of World War I, Hans Dominik and Richard Scherl tweaked the telemobiloscope and built what they called a *Strahlenzieler* (ray pointer). Again the admirals couldn't see the possibilities and said *nein*.

The following year, New York–based Nikola Tesla chimed in again and tried to point the US Navy in the right direction. In an article published in the *Electrical Experimenter* in August 1917, Tesla told an interviewer that "If [a ship] can shoot out a concentrated ray . . . of electrical charges . . . and then intercept this ray, after it has been reflected by a submarine hull for example, and cause this intercepted ray to illuminate a fluorescent screen . . . then our problem of locating the hidden submarine will have been solved." Tesla's biographer Margaret Cheney wrote that if anyone at the US Navy had actually read this article, it "would certainly have been discounted as mere dream stuff."

There was, however, one person who didn't consider it "dream stuff." Guess who? Yes, Guglielmo Marconi had been refining his wireless telegraphy for two decades. In the late spring of 1922, Marconi sailed his 220-foot yacht, *Elettra*, from Southampton, England, to New York City, where he addressed a room full of radio and electrical engineers. During this speech, he reminded the audience that Hertz had proved that electric waves can be completely reflected. "It seems to me," he continued, that "it should be possible to design apparatus" for a ship to transmit radio waves "in any desired direction." If the waves come across a metallic object such as a steamer or ship, said Marconi, they would be reflected to a receiver on the sending ship, "and thereby immediately reveal the presence and bearing of the other ship in fog or thick weather." Marconi's biographer Marc Raboy called this "an astounding announcement." But it was astounding only to people who hadn't read Tesla's article five years earlier.

We don't know whether twenty-one-year-old Leo Young or forty-three-year-old Dr. Albert Hoyt Taylor had read Tesla's article or whether they were in the audience when Marconi discussed signal detection, but we do know that both men were thinking along the same lines.

Leo Young grew up on a farm in rural Van Wert, Ohio, and by the time he was fourteen, he had built his first radio set. He even made his own earphones. After graduating from high school, Young began work as a telegraph operator for the Pennsylvania Railroad. Then came World War I. Being of draft age, Young enlisted in the naval reserve. Good choice. Instead of being drafted into the army and sent overseas to France, Young was sent to the Great Lakes Naval Radio Station near Lake Bluff, Illinois. On his first day of active service, he met Dr. Taylor, who had grown up in Wilmette, Illinois, a few miles north of Chicago. He too was a born tinkerer, and long before entering high school, Taylor was making his own batteries and constructing his own telegraph line.

SAFETY FIRST

In 1909, Guglielmo Marconi shared the Nobel Prize in Physics with Karl Ferdinand Braun, the German who invented the cathode ray oscilloscope. The Ohio-born Wright Brothers (Wilbur and Orville), who invented the airplane in 1903, were nominated for the prize, but according to one historian, the Nobel committee may have been leery about honoring an invention that could be used for military purposes.

After earning a degree in engineering at nearby Northwestern University, Taylor undertook graduate studies in Germany, where he was awarded a PhD in physics. Dr. Taylor spent seven years teaching at the University of North Dakota. When the United States entered World War I in 1917, he took a leave from teaching, joined the naval reserve, and was promptly assigned to the station at Lake Bluff, a location chosen for its proximity to Chicago and water access to the Atlantic Ocean.

Dr. Taylor was tough and highly disciplined, and if someone didn't meet his standards, he would let them know. A colleague recalled that most of the young engineers were terrified of Dr. Taylor walking up behind them while they were working on an experiment. But Leo Young wasn't intimidated. And despite the big difference in age and education, Young and Taylor worked well together. The older man was impressed with Young's ingenuity. A colleague said that Dr. Taylor had "the brains and the ideas," and Young knew how "to follow through with them." After the war, when Dr. Taylor was reassigned to a new naval radio laboratory in Washington, DC, he took Young with him.

In September 1922 (a month after Marconi's speech in New York), the US Navy assigned Young and Dr. Taylor the job of studying new methods of communicating from ship to shore and from ship to ship. Dr. Taylor promptly set up a transmitter in "a little shack on the east side of the Potomac River in Washington, DC." The shack was formally known as the Aircraft Radio Laboratory, Anacostia Naval Air Station. Young drove over a nearby bridge and set up his receiver on the west side of the river, about four thousand nautical feet from the transmitter.

Dr. Taylor transmitted a radio wave, and Young obtained a steady signal until two ships sailed up the Potomac and came between the transmitter and receiver. What happened next validated the theories of Tesla and Marconi. Dr. Taylor wrote, "We noticed that, due to the signals being reflected by passing vessels, we could detect their presence and approximate location." Both men "realized that this phenomenon might be extremely useful" and could be put to work immediately as an alarm system around harbors and among fleet formations.

In his report to the navy's bureau of engineering, Dr. Taylor shared details of the experiment and then requested that he and Young be allowed to put radio wave equipment on two destroyers and take them to sea at night. He wanted to prove that other ships could not "filter" between the two destroyers "without detection." At the time, there was no name for this alarm system, so Young and Dr. Taylor called it "the detection of moving objects by radio." Dr. Taylor pointed out that the system should work under smoky and foggy conditions as well as in darkness, and that he and Young considered it worthy of further investigation.

How much excitement did Dr. Taylor's report generate? Answer: Very little. The navy was more interested in communication than detection, and as a result nobody at the bureau of engineering even bothered to respond to Dr. Taylor's request. Young and Dr. Taylor might have pushed harder or urged their superiors to seek money and manufacturing help from American technology corporations such as Westinghouse, Philco, or Radio Corporation of America (later RCA). But pleas for outside help would likely have gone nowhere for two reasons. First, during the 1920s there was no war to fight, hence no enemy ships or planes to detect. Second, technology corporations were putting their resources into the manufacture of home radios, a new and wildly popular seventy-dollar device that enabled Americans to listen to ball games, concerts, dramas, and opera from the comfort of their homes. The stock market crash of 1929 and the Great Depression of the 1930s did nothing to slow the sale of radios. In 1933, for example, with fourteen million people out of work, Americans still bought more than three and half million radios. But something else happened in 1933 that changed the course of both history and manufacturing. Across the Atlantic, in Germany, forty-three-year-old Adolf Hitler (aided by his violent *Schutzstaffel* or Protection Squads, called SS for short) eliminated his political opponents and seized dictatorial power. Hitler's first priority was modernizing the German military. What before had been a small, secret, and informal rearming operation, Hitler openly and massively expanded.

By 1934, it was clear to the rest of the world that German factories were mass-producing tanks, artillery, and technologically advanced combat aircraft. In August of that year, a British physicist named Frederick Lindemann sent a letter to the *Times* [of London] in which he warned that "bombing aeroplanes in the hands of gangster Governments might jeopardize the whole future of our Western civilization." To do nothing about such a threat, said Lindemann, "is inexcusable." He urged the British government to provide funding so physics, math, and engineering professors could begin searching for new scientific ways to defend Britain against German bombers. A year later the government did just that.

Meanwhile back in the United States, Leo Young had never stopped thinking about radio detection. Despite the navy's indifference, Young continued conducting unauthorized experiments, one of which revealed that an airplane created the same interference pattern as passing ships.

Young sent his observations to Dr. Taylor, who sent the bureau of engineering another plea for funding. "More work remains to be done with transmitters and receivers," he wrote, but radio wave detection is "far enough advanced to warrant much further and intensive investigation." Dr. Taylor also convinced his boss to send a supporting letter stressing the fact that detection of surface ships and aircraft was a "matter of the utmost importance."

Those two letters did the trick. On January 19, 1931, the bureau of engineering gave formal (but grudging) authorization to the radio detection project. The bureau offered no money and no new employees. And neither Dr. Taylor nor Young was assigned to the project on a full-time basis. But finally they had official government approval!

Over the next year, Young and Dr. Taylor continued to experiment with what were known as continuous wave transmissions. Continuous waves are like a waterfall. Great flow, but impossible to isolate a single drop. In late 1933, Young imagined a radio wave system built on a different operating principle. Instead of continuous waves, why not short, sharp pulses? What prompted Young's change in thinking? Transmitting short pulses and timing the return echoes would allow a radio operator to measure the distance to a ship or a plane. Young spent his off-hours investigating the pulse method, and his early findings gave him enough confidence to pitch the idea to Dr. Taylor. The older man was dubious. Could the pulses of the transmitter really synchronize with a time axis on the receiver? What if the receiver was unable to detect such short pulses? Young said he'd find solutions. Taylor easily could have said no and suffered no consequences. Many of Dr. Taylor's colleagues had warned him that the "obvious weaknesses" of the pulse method could not be overcome. In some quarters of the radio division there was "outright antagonism" against funding such a project. But Taylor had faith in his longtime colleague, and he agreed to okay the project on two conditions. First, Young had to team up with a new and well-educated hotshot in the department. His name was Robert Page, and he was a thirty-year-old physicist in the radio division. Second, Young and Page had to show results within six months. Otherwise, said Dr. Taylor, "we'll cancel it out." Though no one knew it at the time, Taylor's okay would prove momentous. A radar historian wrote later, "The decision to try this [pulse] approach was the most important technical choice of the project." And Young's new teammate was just the man for the job.

Robert Morris Page was born in 1903, the seventh of nine children. His first eight years of formal schooling took place in Eden Prairie, Minnesota, where his dad worked as a painter, paperhanger, and farmer. For young Robert the day started at four in the morning, when he and his older brothers helped Dad load up his horse-drawn cart full of produce bound for the markets in Minneapolis.

One of those brothers became an electrician, and when Robert was a teenager, he tagged along to watch his brother work and eventually learned how to wire houses. Robert became familiar with electrical components and made enough money to attend Hamline University in Saint Paul. His plan was to be a clergyman so he could "be of useful service to [his] fellow man." But after realizing he was a "complete flop" at public speaking, he switched to math and physics. It turned out his favorite professor was a friend of Dr. Taylor's, and two weeks after Page received his bachelor of science degree in physics, Taylor offered him a job at the Naval Research Laboratory in Washington. It didn't take long for Page's colleagues to notice that this new guy had a knack for seeing solutions that weren't apparent to others. Dr. Taylor said Page possessed "extraordinary ability and fertility of invention." Another colleague wasn't quite so poetic. He said Page "had more ideas than a dog had fleas."

Leo Young and Robert Page worked on the pulse method through the summer and fall of 1934. Young did the tinkering, and Page did the equations and advanced electrical engineering. "This is what we ought to do," Young would say, "but I don't know how to do it . . . you're the smart guy—you figure it out."

After six months of mental and manual labor, the guys still didn't have a working model. But they were close. Taylor gave them two more months. By mid-December, they had a system they thought might work. It was time for the big test.

Atop two adjacent buildings along the Potomac River, mechanics erected antennas and pointed them toward the water.

In one building, Young revved up the pulse transmitter, and next door Page hunkered down by the receiver, which was connected to a glowing computer-sized screen called an oscilloscope, or "scope" for short. The scope was invented in 1897 by a German electrical engineer named Karl Ferdinand Braun. It was designed to turn electromagnetic echoes into visual images that appear as dots or quarter-inch vertical lines that became known as blips or pips. Page fed power to the equipment and then phoned the nearby airport. As planned, a small airplane took off and flew up and down the Potomac at low altitude through the radio waves.

Page didn't record how long he stared at the scope or how many times he tapped his fingers or his shoes, but at some point, while the transmitter was off in the interval between outgoing pulses, several blips appeared. Well, not exactly blips. More like blobs or smears. The receiver obviously needed more clarity. Nonetheless, wrote Page, pulsed radar passed "its first test with an airplane target in December 1934." There were still some doubters at the radio lab who told Dr. Taylor he was going down a "blind alley." Again Taylor didn't waver. Despite the blobby signal echoes, he said the work "was promising enough to go on." Funding would continue, although radio detection would be classified "extremely low priority."

Within a few days of that first test, Page began diagnosing and correcting the problems. He submitted a reworked design to the engineering shop, where they built and delivered a new receiver in November 1935. It was better than the first version, but there were still deficiencies. Page's logbook for the next few months reports a "series of tests, adjustments, replacement parts, and so on." When funding for radio detection slowed to a trickle, Page and Young resorted to chicanery, reclassifying the receiver as a "communication" device so they could siphon funds from another project. They got away with that deception, and the new equipment was finally ready to be tested in April 1936. "Success came immediately," wrote radar historian David Allison. Random planes were detected at two miles, and "the echoes were clear and distinct. There was no smearing out or fuzziness, and the received pulses were as sharp as those transmitted." It was now clear to Dr. Taylor that radio detection would become a reality.

Since all military research and development was top secret, Young, Page, and Dr. Taylor had no idea what sort of progress other countries were making. Much later they would learn that British scientists had been nipping at their heels. In February 1935, just two months after the first American test, three Brits had hunched over a scope in the back of an old ambulance that had been converted into a mobile signal detection lab. The vehicle was parked in a farmer's field seventy miles north of London. As a Royal Air Force pilot flew overhead, quarter-inch blips flicked on the scope. "I was highly elated," said one of the scientists, who added, "I realized that we were 'on to a good thing' for air defence." Another scientist said it was the most convincing test he had ever witnessed and "demonstrated beyond doubt that electromagnetic energy is reflected from the metal components of an aircraft's structure and that it can be detected." For the next four years, the Americans and British both made significant advances in radio detection, though neither knew what the other was up to.

The first big advances came after construction workers in both countries erected pairs of latticed metal towers, some as tall as a twenty-story building. In Britain, a former meteorologist named Robert Watson-Watt led the radio detection team, and he selected the sites along the east coast of England and Scotland where the towers could beam radio waves over the English Channel and detect incoming threats from Europe. Technicians trained by tracking Dutch and German passenger planes flying from Europe to London.

In the United States, the first towers went up at the naval air station in Washington, DC. At the top of each 200-foot tower was a rectangular antenna about twenty feet long and ten feet high. The towers were built in pairs so one antenna could transmit the radio waves while the other received (or detected) the reflected radio echo. Once a clear radio echo was received, it was sent by electronic circuitry to the scope in the radio room down below. Scientists discovered that significant space was needed between the two antennas so the powerful outgoing transmission wouldn't interfere with or possibly compromise the weaker incoming echo. Page said the distance between towers should be no less than 250 feet.

On June 10, 1936, American radio operators detected test planes twenty miles away. Rear Admiral Harold Bowen, the new head of the navy's bureau of engineering, was so pleased with the results that he upgraded radio detection to "highest possible priority" and raised it from "a confidential to a secret category."

With research and development money suddenly available, Dr. Taylor summoned Young and Page and told them the navy had a problem. Battleships and destroyers bristled with armaments, communication instruments, and naval equipment. There simply wasn't room on the superstructure of such ships to install two antennas. Taylor asked the two men to focus all their energy on building a single antenna capable of transmitting radio waves *and* receiving uncompromised reflections. Not only that, Dr. Taylor wanted Young and Page to oversee a shipboard test of the single antenna "at the earliest possible date."

As they walked out of the office, Page said to Young that building a one-antenna system was "utterly impossible. There is just no way." This man, known to have more ideas than a dog has fleas, had no idea where to begin. You can understand Page's pessimism if you imagine squinting into a powerful searchlight for a second or two and then trying to identify small letters on an eye chart. It's impossible because the brilliant flash of light temporarily impairs your vision. An outgoing wave of energy similarly "blinds" and "destabilizes" an incoming echo. Page said that on a single antenna, the "receiver would be burned up by the transmitter."

"Well, think about it," said Young. "There ought to be a way."

Page did think about it. For several months. According to his son, the idea for the "duplexer" came to Page during a Sunday church service during which "he apparently wasn't paying attention to the minister." While others called it a flash of genius, Page said, "I only followed a 'hunch,' or as I prefer to call it, an inspiration, in which the completed configuration appeared in my imagination without an understanding of how it worked, but with a feeling of great confidence that it would work. It was as if a source of knowledge out of this world had momentarily been opened to me, and I was guided by it."

The key component of this single-antenna apparatus was a switch. It disconnected the receiver when the transmitter sent out pulses, and it disconnected the transmitter as the receiver picked up echoes. Compare this to safety precautions taken by a road crew when they shrink a two-lane road down to one lane. What happens? A person at one end holds up a sign that says, "Stop." The person at the other end holds up a sign that says, "Slow." At timed intervals, they flip their signs. Assuming the correct signs are held up at the right times, the traffic moves through on one lane, and there are no collisions. Likewise, Page's duplexer moved two-way radio wave traffic on one lane and prevented the receiver from being "blinded" or "burned up" by outgoing transmissions.

Page built the duplexer during the summer of 1936. He said, "It worked perfectly the first time it was tried." Historian David Allison noted that "like so many other aspects of the development of radar," the creation of this device resulted from a combination of individual brilliance and teamwork. "Page's inventive talent allowed him to conceive the duplexer," wrote Allison, but only after both

Dr. Taylor and Young pushed Page to reject his initial skepticism and "exercise his talent."

In April 1937, the duplexer was integrated with the transmitter and receiver, and the complete system was tested for the first time. The results were disappointing. No aircraft were detected beyond fifteen miles. The problem, according to Page, was that the pulses from the transmitter were too weak. He and Young went back to work. They, along with several associates, not only rebuilt the transmitter, they also modified the receiver and added a rotating mount so the antenna could spin 360 degrees and "see" in all directions. In his diary, Page noted that these improvements were "completed on the 17th day of Feb. 1938." A few months later, a land-based test of the new system "equaled our dreams," wrote Page. It even tracked an old biplane with a wooden fuselage and fabric wings, the same elements on a raft with a sail. Young and Page concluded that the equipment was ready to go to sea, and on December 8, 1938, the first American shipboard radio detection system was installed on the battleship USS *New York*, which was then undergoing an overhaul at the Norfolk Navy Yard in Virginia.

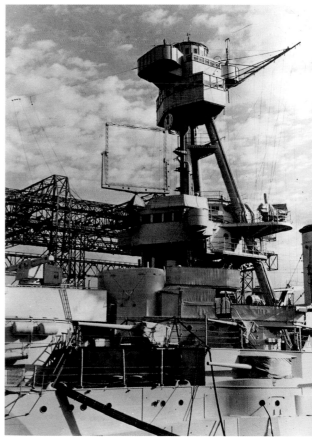

The USS **New York** *with radar antenna— the ship was the first to have an onboard radar detection system*

Young positioned the seventeen-foot-square rotating antenna just forward of the ship's foremast, eighty feet above the waterline. Sailors watching the installation were told nothing about the secret device, but there was plenty of speculation. Many referred to the antenna as the "flying bedspring." In early 1939, during fleet exercises in the Caribbean, it was put to the test. According to Page, who was on board the *New York*, the results of the test were "spectacular." Buoys were observed at four miles, ships at ten miles, aircraft at fifty miles, and neither high winds, rain storms, nor the shock of gunfire interfered with the outgoing or incoming signals. Following these fleet exercises, the commanding officer of the *New York*, Captain R. M. Griffin, wrote that by "standing guard against surprise," this new device would have "far reaching effects on tactics." He recommended that the equipment immediately "be installed on all aircraft carriers and as soon as practicable on other vessels." He urged his fellow officers not to quibble about the size of the antenna. "The device looks big," he wrote, "but really caused very little inconvenience. After all, we can't expect to get something for nothing. It is well worth the space it occupies."

The next year, 1940, was a big one for radio wave detection. First, two US Navy officers coined the word radar. Second, with the help of radar (and detailed preparation), three thousand UK

HELP WANTED

Beginning in late 1941, American newspapers began running articles with the following headline: "Navy Needs Operators for 'Radar.'" One such article continued:

"'Radar.'

What is it?

S-s-sh! That's a secret.

But it isn't a secret that the Navy wants 5,000 amateur radio operators and radio service men for training in handling this new confidential equipment."

Royal Air Force pilots defeated Hitler's *Luftwaffe* in the skies over Britain. This was Germany's first defeat of the war, and without control of the skies, Hitler had to cancel his long-planned, cross-channel invasion of England, Scotland, and Ireland. Third, radar equipment was installed on more than twenty US warships. And fourth, Britain and the United States finally agreed to share their radar secrets with each other. When a British scientist disclosed that he had figured out how to fit an entire radar system on an airplane, mechanical and electrical engineers of the US Navy wasted no time copying the British model and installing the two-hundred-pound systems on American aircraft. In June 1942, airborne radar had played a key role in the American victory at the Battle of Midway in the South Pacific. At the same time in the South Atlantic, Lieutenant Donald Gay and his eighty-five-man squadron of naval aviators began flying radar-equipped PBY seaplanes (patrol bombers) on ten-to-fifteen-hour reconnaissance missions over the waters east of Trinidad. They were looking for surfaced U-boats or any survivors of torpedo attacks. Gay recalled, "We were one of the early squadrons to be equipped with radar . . . we could 'see' surfaced submarines and ships at distances up to twelve miles." Rafts and lifeboats were harder to detect, but the long odds of such a sighting didn't stop Gay's men from flying thousands of hours over an endless expanse of open water.

On September 6, 1942, Lieutenant Gay received a formal report that listed the *West Lashaway* as "delayed, perhaps missing." The ship's last known latitude and longitude appeared in an encoded ship-to-shore communication on August 29, the day before the *West Lashaway* was sunk.

"Well, that gives us some idea of where to look," said Gay to a fellow navy flier. "Let's get a couple of more men and go searching."

CHAPTER 10

GOING SOLO

AFTER FIVE DAYS of drifting, Captain Bogdan decided that linking the four rafts together had been a mistake. In rough seas the rafts either jerked apart or smashed together, and woe to anyone whose fingers were caught in a collision. The captain also thought that splitting up would increase the odds of a raft being spotted. Bogdan motioned for Greenwell and spoke to him in a voice inaudible to anyone else on the raft. Greenwell nodded and said, "I agree, captain."

"Give the men my orders, Mr. Greenwell."

"Aye, aye, sir." Greenwell stood up, and to keep his balance he held on to one of the oars that supported the mast. After signaling to the other rafts to pull closer, he shouted, "Listen up, everybody. Captain Bogdan's decided it's best for us to cut the lines and go our separate ways." He explained the captain's thinking and then said, "Woodman, you got your knife handy?"

"Yes sir, Mr. Greenwell."

"There was no discussion, no questioning the decision, no protest," Robert wrote. "Everyone seemed content with the captain's wisdom, even though we knew what separating might mean." Records don't indicate whether there was any redistribution of food or water.

Potter started with the farthest raft and worked his way back. He also cut loose the floating mattress contraption.

There were shouts of "Good luck!" and "See you in New York!" Earlier Mr. Shaw had told his son, Richard, "to take good care of Carol."

Mary recalled each raft rising and falling on the crests of the waves. "We'd go up and down at different times, flowing through a trough and entirely out of sight of the other rafts. Then, suddenly, we'd pitch upward, and there we'd see one or another of the rafts. But each time they came back into view, we were farther and farther away. For me it was very depressing to watch the other rafts disappear."

"I was numb," recalled Richard Shaw. "I remember watching Dad's raft drift away, watching it get smaller and smaller, until it was gone, and he wasn't there anymore. It happened so fast."

Robert's only recollection of the next several days was "that nothing happened." Same weather, same rations, same quiet, same stiff back, same chilly nights. "Remember," said Greenwell, "some of us barely had any clothes on. Me, I had only my skivvies and a burlap bag that itched me all day and did little to warm me at night. It was like an ice box out there." It wasn't just the chill that made the nights rough. "I fell backward one night," recalled Marano, "but I managed to straighten myself up before I hit the water. The first thing I had on my mind was those sharks." Even when people slept, it was never a deep sleep. "You knew where you were, and yet you didn't know," said Marano. "It was like a blankness of the mind, or maybe a way of easing up on the reality of our situation." There was also the fear of U-boats that surfaced at night to run their generators and recharge their batteries. "One time we passed so close to a sub, we could hear conversation and laughter from the deck," recalled Greenwell. "Another time there were two tied up together. We could hear their iron hulls grating against each other and see the string of lights . . . that marked the walkways. But they never saw us in the dark."

By week two, some of the rafters were so hungry they began scooping up and eating the little fish that swam through the slats and into the well of the raft. Those minnow "appetizers" got Potter thinking about bigger fish, specifically the foot-long pilot fish that accompany sharks and feast on leftovers.

Potter took a safety pin out of the first aid kit, bent it into a hook, and said he was "going a-fishing." With great care and concentration, he unraveled the strands of a thick hemp rope and then wove several of those thin strands into a fishing line. "The children found a never-ending delight in watching him," wrote Mrs. Bell. Potter swiped up a minnow and stuck it on the hook. He flipped the fishing line over the side of the raft and waited for a nibble. As he sat there, Potter began singing, "You are my sunshine, my only sunshine," and carried on through the recent hit song.

After finishing, he sang a second solo. The third time, three others joined him. By the fourth round, everyone was singing

CLEANUP ON AISLE ONE

U-boats surfaced for both mechanical and health reasons. Fresh air was a gift to crewmen who spent days, weeks, and months in a narrow metal tube that reeked of body odor, human waste, moldy food, battery gas, and diesel oil. One historian described a U-boat as "a sewer pipe with valves." There were only two bathrooms for fifty men. For the first week or two at sea, one bathroom was unusable because it was crammed with crates of fresh fruit. Until that was eaten, crew members had to be careful to operate the one toilet correctly. Various valves had to be opened and closed in the correct order, and the end product, after traveling through two interior compartments, had to be flushed into the ocean using a hand pump. Upon exiting the bathroom, a sailor signed a clipboard hung on the door. If there was a clogged pipe, the offender was called to clean up.

except the bosun. Even the captain managed a few words. Potter caught no fish that first day. Nor did he catch any on the second or third day. But each day, he led a sing-along that probably did more for morale than a few bites of fish would've.

"Just as the food game had helped to sustain us during the first week," said Robert, "so now it was singing that became our tonic." This became even more vital after the "Angel of Death" visited the raft—twice.

On September 7 (day nine on the raft), the Angel came for "Flags" Koonz. "I think he must have been hurt internally when the ship was torpedoed," wrote Mrs. Bell. She added, "His end was peaceful and without pain, as far as we could judge. . . . There was silence on the raft that morning. Death is always a solemn thing."

Captain Bogdan was in no condition to conduct a burial service, so Greenwell asked Mrs. Bell to say a few words. "What could I do?" she wondered. "I had neither prayer book nor Bible and knew nothing of the life or beliefs of the deceased." She cleared her throat and said, "Men, I'm not able to pray for Mr. Koonz. His soul is in God's hands and in God's destiny. But I can pray for each of us [as we] face the unknown future, with all that it might hold." Mrs. Bell wrote that she "prayed briefly," asking the "Heavenly Father" for help, support, and strength.

THE SINGING GOVERNOR

The song "You Are My Sunshine" is one of the most popular in American history. Two people claim credit for writing it. One is Paul Rice, whose band, the Rice Brothers Gang, recorded the song in 1939. Music historians claim that Rice sold the song rights for thirty-five dollars to Jimmie Davis, a college professor and country western singer. Davis and band leader Charles Mitchell made the song a hit for Decca Records in 1940, and both men's names were listed on the copyright.

Greenwell and Marano gently removed Flags's shirt and pants and handed them to people who needed more clothing. They swaddled Flags in burlap and rolled him overboard. Mrs. Bell told her children not to look. They didn't, but they could still hear the violent thrashing as the sharks converged, ripped apart the burlap, and stained the ocean red.

Two days later, on September 9 just after sunrise, Captain Bogdan summoned Greenwell, pulled him close, and whispered, "They mustn't get the gold, Mr. Greenwell. . . . The Germans mustn't get the Frenchman's fifty million in gold."

"It's all right, Captain Bogdan," whispered Greenwell. "The gold went down with the ship."

"With the ship? The ship's sinking you say?"

"The ship's been sunk for more than a week, Captain."

"We've got to save the ship! Save the gold!"

"It's too late to save the ship, Captain. . . . We've got to save ourselves now. Just relax, sir."

Bogdan had one more thing on his mind. "If I am relieved, Mr. Greenwell, I want you to take command."

"Yes, sir."

"You're sure they didn't get the Frenchman's gold?"

"Sir, nobody got it. It all went to the bottom."

In later years, Davis claimed he alone had written the music and lyrics. When Davis ran for Louisiana governor in 1944, he used the song as his campaign theme, "singing it during stump speeches and at fundraisers, often while riding a horse he had named 'Sunshine.'" He won and served one term. Twenty years later he used the same song and won the governorship again. There are now more than 350 versions in thirty languages. In 1972, Davis was elected to the Country Music Hall of Fame in Nashville.

An hour later, Captain Bogdan succumbed to his internal injuries. "For a moment or two there was silence," wrote Mrs. Bell, "broken only by the low, soft moaning of the sea as it sang a requiem to the one who had gone."

Greenwell said, "He was one of the finest men I ever knew." Robert guessed that the captain's pain must have been excruciating all along, "yet never once did he allow himself the normal man's expression of suffering. He was a superb example of personal courage on behalf of us all."

As before, the men turned to Mrs. Bell, who spoke as much of the burial service as she could recall and ended her remarks with a plea to God to "watch over us" and "bring us to safety soon." Once again, the men slid the much-needed clothing off the deceased man, even though salt water had rotted away much of the fabric. It was just after nine o'clock in the morning when the captain was consigned to the deep.

Losing Captain Bogdan was a "serious blow to our morale," said Robert. Despite Bogdan's injuries and his frailty, his presence had "meant something." As long as he was aboard the raft, "the men would obey any command of his; there'd be order and routine. Now, with him dead, we worried what might happen."

Barely an hour after the burial service, Peifer said, "Listen up, you guys. Captain Bodgan was a good man and all that, but he was too hurt to give us the kind of leadership we need. Now that he's dead, I don't propose that we should be without a leader any longer. So I'm declaring myself in command of this raft. I'm the best organizer here, and from the looks of things, I'm also in the best shape. So, from now on, you take your orders from me."

"Says who, Peifer?" barked Greenwell. Navy rules specified the bosun was in command of the crew but not the officers. "I'm the senior officer on board," said Greenwell.

"Yea, but you haven't done nothin' but play nursemaid to the captain," said Peifer. "I'm the real leader here, and everyone knows it." Before Greenwell could answer, Peifer added, "Okay, Mrs. Bell, I want you and the kids to get into the doughnut."

"You must be kidding," said Marano. "That thing is hardly big enough for two men. You're not putting a woman and four children in it! Can't be done!"

"These rafts were made for officers and crew," said Peifer, "not for friggin' women and children."

"Don't pay any attention to him, Mrs. Bell," said Marano. "He's all talk."

"Shut up, Marano. You heard me, Mrs. Bell," said Peifer, pointing to the dinghy.

Robert gripped his mother's arm.

Peifer stared at Mrs. Bell and waited.

"He was determined to harm us," said Mary.

Mrs. Bell stared back at the bosun and said, "Mr. Peifer, I refuse to move."

Potter cheered her response. "Don't never get in that doughnut, Mrs. Bell," he said. "He'll cut you loose without rations."

Before Peifer could respond, a rainbow suddenly appeared on the horizon. Mrs. Bell was quick to point to the sky. "God's message of hope to us," she said. "He takes our tears, like raindrops, and by the sunlight of His love . . . turns them into something beautiful."

Peifer shouted, "God—God—God—God! That's all I hear, is *God!* . . . We're stuck out here in the middle of the ocean, and all you and this fool woman and her brats can blab about is God! Well, let me tell you something once and for all. There is no God! I'm the only God I'll ever know or need." He turned toward the messmen. "You want to be alive when this raft is found? . . . Act like men, use your heads like I do, and we've got a chance. . . . Go on singing and praying, and we'll all be dead!"

Peifer waited. No one responded. To move Mrs. Bell and the children off the raft and into the doughnut, Peifer needed accomplices. He couldn't take on everyone alone. Hoping to sway Chico, Seramos, and Flavor, Peifer pointed at those three and said, "You mark my words. You'll regret the day you let these five take your rations and your space." But they were not swayed. Neither were the other crewmen.

As Peifer contemplated his next move, Mrs. Bell began to sing a hymn.

> *"Unto the hills around do I lift up*
> *My longing eyes.*
> *O whence for me shall my salvation come?*
> *From whence arise?"*

The bosun shook his head, grumbled, and said no more. That night Potter thought he saw a glow in the darkness. "I was scared, I looked up, and I believe I saw a light over the raft!" He later told Mrs. Bell, "That light was your faith, and it saved us."

On Sunday, September 13, the survivors began their third week on the raft. Not wishing to provoke Peifer, Mrs. Bell made no mention of a church service. Instead she and the children quietly recited a few biblical passages. Afterward Mrs. Bell struggled to her feet and tried to exercise by lifting one foot, then the other. "But even this mild exercise became too painful, since my feet and legs were so swollen with sores from long immersion in salt water."

The bosun said nothing until late afternoon, when rations were distributed. "Listen, everybody. We're getting low on food," Peifer said. "Starting tomorrow, it's one meal a day, so eat up now. We won't have rations again until sundown tomorrow."

The weight of those words had barely sunk in when the rafters heard the drone of an airplane engine. "I don't remember who saw it first," wrote Robert, "but all of a sudden, that Sunday evening, there was a PBY directly overhead." Mrs. Bell wrote, "We could see men looking down on us from the windows." Everyone struggled to their feet. Some shouted and laughed, others cried and shook hands with each other. "We . . . probably would have danced for joy had there been room," wrote Mrs. Bell. There was so much movement that one side of the raft tilted down toward the waterline. "Easy does it!" shouted the bosun. "Let's not dump this damned thing. We still got company out there in the water."

The plane circled several times before one of the pilots dropped a box that "struck the water like a brick" and broke apart about twenty feet from the raft. The rafters watched helplessly as sandwiches floated in all directions and were quickly gobbled up by the sharks. The pilots saw the mishap and made a second pass. "Down it came," wrote Mrs. Bell, "almost in a straight dive" before flattening out about fifty feet above the raft. Mary wrote that the plane came in so low "we could see the airmen's faces."

This time the bundle that fell from the plane was wrapped in a yellow waterproof canvas that held tight as it smacked the water. Mary said these were "probably their own emergency rations." The bosun told Chico to shimmy into the doughnut and get the goodies. As Chico paddled, the PBY circled back and made a third drop, this one wrapped in a life jacket. Chico returned with the two precious parcels, which contained four tins of condensed milk, three tins of pemmican, a tin each of Spam and corned beef, a note that said "Trinidad," and of all things, two dresses. "The airmen must have seen Mother and me," wrote Mary. "We didn't get [to wear them] though as they were quickly taken by men whose clothing was in worse shape than ours." The PBY flew off. Mary thought that "the plane's crew would certainly send help the next day."

"That night," wrote Mrs. Bell, "we dined royally. For the first time in fourteen days everyone had enough to eat and drink. The corned beef and Spam were like ambrosia," she recalled, "and the drink of condensed milk (which all received) will linger long in my memory." When the milk ran out, the rafters guzzled water, one glass after another.

"Do you think we ought to use up all the water?" someone asked.

"Why not? We're not gonna need it tomorrow."

"Drink up, shipmates!" Then came the rousing toasts.

"Here's to the United States Navy!"

"Here to Chico for pullin' in the drops!"

"Here's to the bosun for grabbin' the doughnut in the first place."

As the feasting and toasting concluded, two crewmen took down the sail so the raft wouldn't drift too far from where they'd been spotted by the airmen.

Mrs. Bell wrote that soon there would be "a chair to sit in . . . a bed to lie in . . . soothing salve for the raw sores on our feet. Do you wonder that we were merry that night, that few of us even thought of trying to sleep?"

Dawn. The rafters' fifteenth morning at sea. "We had our prayers and breakfast," wrote Mrs. Bell. Those facing westward scanned the sky hoping to see the PBY that would drop a string of smoke lights to guide the nearest ship to the survivors. Rafters could hear the distant drone of plane engines, but no PBY came into view. Half an hour passed before a long gray ship appeared on the horizon and began trolling back and forth, "obviously search-ing," wrote Mary. Someone identified it as a US destroyer. Robert wrote there were only "two or three miles separating the raft from deliverance." The ship rose higher as it approached. "We watched and waited in an agony of suspense," wrote Mrs. Bell, "torn between hopes and fears." But with no PBY to guide the ship, it suddenly turned and took a course away from the raft.

"Hey, what's goin' on?" asked one of the men.

"Over here!" shouted another.

"Damn you, open your eyes!"

All morning the ship swept in wide arcs. "We could tell [they were] looking for us," wrote Robert, but they didn't realize "how small a speck our raft must have been." Mrs. Bell recalled feeling "a sickening of the heart" as the ship turned away and got smaller and smaller until "only a smudge of smoke" hovered over the distant horizon. Mary wrote that when the ship disappeared, it took with it "our hopes and spirits."

There were two likely reasons why no PBY appeared and why the ship's radarman saw no blip on his scope. One, the rafters had taken down the sail, which left the raft with a barely discernible silhouette. Two, the radar equipment on the PBY and on the ship had not yet been upgraded. It was still the 1941 version—radar 1.0, if you will.

Years later, navy flier Lieutenant Donald Gay described radar 1.0 as "very primitive, still experimental." Then he revealed how he became part of the experiment.

WWII-era cavity magnetron, capable
of transmitting microwaves, overlaid
with microwave lines

CHAPTER 11

MICROWAVES

AT TWO FORTY in the morning on August 29, 1942, the US Navy base in Trinidad received a distress call from the *Topa Topa,* an American cargo ship torpedoed while sailing from Trinidad to Takoradi, Gold Coast, and Lagos, Nigeria. The following day, five hours before the *West Lashaway* was hit, another distress call came in from the *Sir Huon*, an American cargo ship en route from South Africa to Trinidad. The navy was able to track these two calls to a grid about 10 degrees north of the equator and slightly west of 50 degrees west longitude, which is a stretch of ocean roughly 450 miles due east of Trinidad. When those coordinates were relayed to patrol squadron 31, Lieutenant Donald Gay and his copilot took off, followed by Lieutenant Tom Evert and his copilot.

The normal search routine was for two PBYs to fly side by side before veering off from each another to scan a square of ocean. If that side trip revealed nothing (as it usually did), the pilots linked up again, waved to each other, and repeated the process. Several hours into the patrol, on one of his side trips, Gay saw a blip on his radar screen. He radioed Evert, who saw a blip as well. Both banked sharply and dove at the target, which they thought was a surfaced U-boat. Only as they roared toward each other did the pilots realize the blips were, in fact, echoes from the other guy's plane! They came so close, said Gay, that "our wings overlapped."

What caused this close call was the ever-widening diameter of the outgoing radar beam. Compare it to a light beam emitted by a flashlight. Stand close to a wall and turn on a flashlight, and the beam is narrow and bright. Back away from the wall, and the light beam widens into a cone and becomes less intense. When such widening happens with radar, the outgoing signals become weaker, and the return echoes from distant targets become so indistinct that it's difficult to figure out in which direction a target is moving. Improving radar 1.0 meant narrowing and concentrating the outgoing electromagnetic beam so it functioned more like a spotlight than a flashlight.

Radar scientists agreed there was only one way to narrow a radar beam: shrink the distance between outgoing electromagnetic waves. That distance is called a wavelength. It's measured from the crest of one wave to the crest of the next wave. In the open ocean, watery wavelengths average between two hundred and five hundred feet. A few hundred feet between waves means a little rest between one breaker and the next. But radar operators didn't want several hundred feet between electromagnetic waves. They wanted one wave immediately after another. A higher frequency of waves means more electromagnetic energy in the outgoing beam. The more outgoing energy, the more vivid the incoming reflections, and the more a radar operator can "see."

By 1940 American scientists and their British counterparts both knew that the only way to generate "a radio wave spotlight" was to build a transmitter capable of sending out electromagnetic waves separated not by feet but by inches. They needed *micro*waves. (Not the boxy appliance in your kitchen, but the four-inch waves that make it work.) The problem was that generating microwaves required an enormous amount of energy. Why? Think about the energy used to take one long step. Compare that to the energy needed to cover the same distance with thirty tiny steps. Microwaves are all those little, high-frequency steps, and it takes more energy to create them.

American scientists were stymied in their attempts to create a microwave transmitter small enough to fit into an airplane. Imagine their surprise when in September 1940, as part of the secret American/British exchange, a British physicist named Edward Bowen brought to Washington, DC, a device so small it could fit into a backpack. Called a cavity magnetron, the device could produce enough energy to transmit microwaves thirty to forty miles! When one American scientist saw the power this little machine generated, he said, "If automobiles had been similarly improved, modern cars would . . . go a thousand miles on a gallon of gas." President Franklin Roosevelt called it "the most valuable cargo ever brought to our shores."

How had the Brits done it? One of the inventors of the cavity magnetron, thirty-four-year-old physics professor John Randall of Birmingham University, said inspiration came to him during a summer vacation in 1939. Randall, his wife, and his young son had gone to the seaside town of Aberystwyth in Wales. One rainy afternoon when the usual beach activities weren't an option, Randall went into town and popped into a bookstore that sold new, used, and out-of-print editions. Browsing through the science section, he spotted a translation of an old Heinrich Hertz book that included a chapter about his now-famous 1886 spark-gap experiment. Randall bought the book and started reading "with some interest in view of our coming radar activities." Hertz's breakthrough, Randall said, "stuck in my mind."

Back at the university, Randall urged his twenty-two-year-old lab partner, Henry Boot, to read the Hertz book. Once Boot completed his "homework," the two men discussed what might happen if they built a device with not one spark-gap but eight. What would a Hertz-times-eight device look like? Randall made sketches, and once they settled on a design, Boot began building a prototype. He started with a ten-inch-square copper block—copper because it was a good conductor of heat, and most good heat conductors are also good conductors of electricity. In the center of the block, Boot drilled a cylindrical hole. Around that central cavity he drilled eight more cavities, each connected to the center one by a narrow stem. From above, it resembled eight lollipops spoking out from a central circle. The lollipop stems were the eight spark-gaps, each one a three-dimensional version of Hertz's wire loop receiver.

Boot calculated the diameter of the "lollipops" using an equation formulated by Hertz: one wavelength of electromagnetic energy is equal to 7.94 times a loop's diameter. The wavelengths of microwaves must be less than ten centimeters (about four inches). Boot rounded up Hertz's 7.94 to 8 and used some simple algebra to figure out that the diameter of each of the six "lollipops" should be 1.2 centimeters. A wire running to the central cylinder supplied the electric current, and a magnet Boot placed under the copper block supplied the magnetic force. Once the power was turned on, the magnetic field caused the electrons to bounce back and forth in the cavities, spark the eight gaps, and generate energy in the form of radio waves.

PRECIOUS CARGO

The cavity magnetron's journey to the United States began on August 29, 1940. English scientist Edward Bowen entered a first-class rail car at London's Euston Station and put the black box containing the magnetron on the luggage rack. The only other person in the car was a trim, well-dressed gentleman who sat diagonally opposite from Bowen. When someone else tried to enter the car, that man barked, "Out! . . . this is specially reserved." Those are the only words he spoke. Upon arrival in Liverpool, two uniformed

Randall and Boot tested their cavity magnetron in a Birmingham University basement on February 21, 1940. Seconds after the power was turned on, observers could see that the output wire was "clothed in a sizzling blue electric discharge." A fellow professor held a cigarette in the beam of radiation. Not only did the cigarette light, but the professor's hand "became uncomfortably warm." Word of the test spread throughout the building, and within half an hour, the chairman of the physics department, Mark Oliphant, arrived in the basement and suggested that Boot wire the magnetron to an automobile headlight, "in an attempt to determine just how much power was being produced." Randall was "hoping they might at least get a dim illumination." That didn't happen. Instead, the headlight brightened, flickered, and burned out. The magnetron was generating too much microwave energy. The same burnout happened to "lamps of successively higher power."

"We were astonished," said Randall. The only thing that didn't burn out was a set of neon floodlights, and when it remained lit, Randall and Boot were able to measure both the wavelength and the power output. The wavelength was just what they had calculated: 9.8 centimeters. The power output was four times the output of existing airborne radar sets, but "it was an easy step to increase the power a hundred-fold!"

men entered the rail car, took possession of the black box, and carried it onto the bridge of the steamship *Duchess of Richmond*. The black box was guarded day and night, and the captain had orders to throw the magnetron overboard if the ship was torpedoed. It wasn't. When the ship arrived in Halifax, Nova Scotia, Canada, soldiers delivered the box to a US Army vehicle that had "submachine guns bristling from every orifice." This vehicle carried the box on its final leg to Washington, DC.

British author Brian Johnson wrote, "It is impossible to exaggerate the importance of Randall and Boot's work." Their cavity magnetron lifted radar out of the "electronic stone age." Historian Ronald Clark noted, "That day in February 1940 can fairly be classed as a turning point in the war." Three months later a British magnetron-powered radar set detected a two-inch-wide submarine periscope seven miles away!

After the information exchange in 1940, Dr. Bowen remained in the United States to help the Americans establish a top-secret microwave radar lab at Massachusetts Institute of Technology (nicknamed the Rad Lab). Retired Cambridge policemen were hired to patrol the hallways and stand guard at the entrances to Building 6 on the MIT campus. In early January 1941, scientists and engineers built the Rad Lab's first microwave radar system on the roof of the building. According to lab lore, the first echo received was from the dome of the Christian Science Mother Church on Massachusetts Avenue in Boston, 1.6 miles away. Two months later, in the skies above Cape Cod, Massachusetts, an American B-18 bomber equipped with microwave radar picked up a target plane two miles away. It was "the first confirmed air-to-air detection in US microwave radar history."

The physicists, engineers, and mathematicians at the Rad Lab established strong links with their counterparts at American technology corporations. When millions of dollars in government funding began flowing to these corporations, hundreds of technicians were hired to assemble the microwave radar components that would be shipped to war-torn Britain and to American military bases around the globe. This unique partnership of government, industry, and academia proved critical to the Allied war effort.

By 1942 hundreds of British and American warships were equipped with the spanking-new magnetron-powered model-271 microwave radar. One of the British ships was the HMS *Vimy*, an old destroyer outfitted with extra fuel tanks and converted into a long-range escort. *Vimy* spent the early summer of 1942 escorting British and American supply ships on a north-south route that took her back and forth between Portsmouth, England; Freetown, Sierra Leone; and Cape Town, South Africa. On August 13, 1942, after arriving in Freetown, the commander of the *Vimy* was ordered to stay put and await further orders.

Remember that the *West Lashaway* departed Takoradi, Gold Coast, on August 15. If you look at a map of West Africa, you'll see that a ship departing Takoradi bound for Trinidad would likely hug the coast of West Africa at least as far north as Sierra Leone before veering west across the Atlantic. Assuming Captain Bogdan took such a route, the *West Lashaway* would have sailed within sight of the ports of Monrovia in Liberia and Freetown in Sierra Leone on or around August 19. It's tempting to imagine Mrs. Bell and one or more of the children leaning on the rail of the *West Lashaway* staring at the very ship that one month later would heave into view and head directly toward their raft.

But before that could happen, the *Vimy* had to pull a new assignment, and the rafters needed help from Mother Nature.

MAKING WAVES

Edward Bowen made a trip to Boston in October 1940 timed to coincide with an MIT conference about applied nuclear physics. One of the luncheons was at a private club. Bowen arrived and used a secret entrance. He was joined by a select group of about two dozen American scientists. None of them had a clue why they were asked to sign a secrecy agreement. Bowen then revealed that he was there to recruit scientists for a secret microwave radar lab at MIT. The next day, the scientists went back to their universities, closed their labs, and found substitute professors for their classes. Many of the scientists who spent 1941 and 1942 working at the secret microwave lab at MIT later worked at the secret atomic bomb laboratory in New Mexico. You can see why World War II was called "the physicists' war."

CHAPTER 12
ANSWERED PRAYERS

DAY SIXTEEN. Luckily for the rafters, they hadn't drunk all the water. According to Mary, there were "less than two gallons left"; that is, less than 256 fluid ounces. The bosun said each person would be allotted two ounces per day: that's four tablespoons, or a quarter cup. After sipping their two ounces, some men begged for a "wee drop more," but the bosun wouldn't allow it. Others began swirling sea water in their mouths to relieve the dryness. But this was "a dangerous practice," wrote Mrs. Bell, "since one's last state would inevitably be worse than the first, and madness lay at the end if no relief were obtained."

On day seventeen, the bosun cut everyone's daily food ration to one cracker and a third of a can of pemmican. Mrs. Bell wrote, "Food had almost lost its interest for me, particularly the dry crackers, which I found impossible to chew owing to the lack of moisture in my mouth."

On day eighteen, the rafters sat under blue skies and a merciless sun. Not until midafternoon did a cloud float into view on the eastern horizon. As it drifted westward, it darkened. The bosun said it was too far away to hope for a desperately needed dousing. One of the crewmen urged Mrs. Bell to "ask God to send the cloud our way and so give us rain." She almost smiled "at the naivete of the request."

Mrs. Bell could have reminded the men that God was not "a convenience to be used in time of danger and distress," but rather a "gracious Being to be loved and served." But this was no time for a theological discussion. So Mrs. Bell "asked our heavenly Father to please send us rain if that was His will; to turn the clouds in our direction."

Each man watched that cloud like a cat watches a caged bird. A half hour went by. The cloud came closer. The men guessed the distance. The wind freshened. The waves kicked up. As the cloud gained speed, some of the men prayed while others spoke to the cloud to urge it on, and then a billowing blackness blotted out the sun and "the windows of heaven were opened."

Every storm at sea was difficult to withstand on the raft

"I had seen tropical rains in Africa," Robert said, "but never anything like this."

"It pelted our faces until it hurt," wrote Mrs. Bell, "and ran through our hair and down our cheeks in a blessed stream of life-giving refreshment." Mary and her mom stood up and stretched out a piece of canvas. Potter cut a hole in the middle, turning it into a funnel. Men sat under the canvas to catch the rainwater in hats, pemmican tins, and drinking cups and dumped it into the water kegs. "Every few minutes," wrote Mrs. Bell, "they would cease these operations long enough to pass around a drink for everyone. Over and over again we enjoyed the luxury of a brimming cupful—and still it poured without cessation." With the first keg filled, they started on the second. Those without containers caught water in their cupped hands and trouser cuffs, and others sat back, tilted their heads, and let the rain fall into their open mouths. It rained until the second keg was nearly full.

As suddenly as the storm had begun, wrote Mrs. Bell, the rain stopped, the sun reappeared, and "we basked in its radiance and warmth until our clothes were again partially dry. All were greatly impressed by this signal answer to prayer and the hearts of some, at least, were thrilled with gratitude and praise."

Hearts were also thrilled the next day when Potter caught two foot long pilot fish. Rodriguez skinned them, extracted the backbones, and divided the fish into seventeen neat squares. Then he

Potter caught two pilot fish to help feed those on the raft

cut the squares in half so everybody could enjoy two pieces. Mrs. Bell had never eaten raw fish before, but she nonetheless eagerly seized her share and devoured it "with relish." As did Carol Shaw. Interviewed seventy years later, Carol said, "I do not remember the fear; I don't remember being scared, I don't really even remember asking about my parents." But she did "remember eating raw fish and liking it." Unfortunately Potter "caught no more fish," wrote Mrs. Bell, but those few bites gave everyone the boost of energy they were about to need.

September in the South Atlantic is hurricane season. A few hours after they enjoyed the sashimi, the sky took on an "angry hue," the winds picked up, and the waves rose. What followed was twelve hours of terror as the little raft repeatedly rode up the side of thirty-foot waves, teetered for a second on the crest, and then plunged down into the trough where the next wall of water blotted out the sky. Sometimes the raft spun as it plunged. Other times it became airborne and people "floated temporarily" before the raft thudded back into the foam. Blinded by sea spray and tumbling walls of water, each person gripped some part of the raft or clung to the next person. Every jerk and bump sent stabbing pains through swollen ankles and saltwater sores. Incredibly, no one was flung into the churning sea, the ropes held the supply chest in place, and the little raft remained upright and intact.

TOGETHER, WHEREVER WE GO

Sharks and pilot fish have what marine biologists call a mutualistic relationship. Sharks shoo predators away from the pilot fish, and in return the fish perform body and dental work on the sharks. They nibble parasites that cling to the shark, and after a shark dines on, say, a seal, the pilot fish swims into the shark's mouth and eats the small pieces of seal flesh stuck between the shark's teeth.

As the storm petered out, the seas gradually grew calm, and the rafters went limp and unclenched their aching fingers for the first time in hours. Peifer asked Chico and Seramos to help him put the sail back up. That bit of business done, everyone sat in silence until Flavor claimed he smelled chili and demanded Rodriguez give him a portion. When the cook said he had no chili, Flavor accused him of lying and lunged toward him. Vega grabbed Flavor by the arm, pulled him back, spoke to him in Spanish, and managed to calm him. It was obvious, wrote Mrs. Bell, "that some were at the breaking point." Robert feared what might happen when the food ran out. Would everyone revert to "animal impulses"? As if reading Robert's mind, a crewman muttered, "We're done for." Another replied, "Don't talk like that." The first man said, "What am I supposed to say? *Any day now?* We ain't got that many days left! Look at us."

If help was arriving, it had better be soon.

The only known photograph of the raft after it was found by the HMS Vimy, overlaid with radar waves

CHAPTER 13
DESTINATION TRINIDAD

TWENTY-FIVE DAYS earlier on August 22, 1942, the captain of the *Vimy*, Henry Graham de Chair, had received his new orders: escort the battered British warship HMS *Queen Elizabeth* (*QE*) from Freetown, Sierra Leone, across the Atlantic to the American navy yard at Norfolk, Virginia. With British ports still subject to occasional German bombing raids, warships in need of major repairs were sent to the United States. Joining the *Vimy* on escort duty were two other British destroyers, the HMS *Pathfinder* and the HMS *Quentin*. After delivering the *QE* to the Americans, the *Vimy* and her sister ships were to head south through the Caribbean to Trinidad, where she would be assigned an escort duty on an eastbound convoy. De Chair wrote that on the Atlantic crossing, the three escorts "proceeded to zigzag at 16 knots [18 miles per hour] most of the way to hamper submarine attacks."

On September 3, at four o'clock on a moonlit morning, an American relief escort met these British ships off the coast of Norfolk, Virginia. "Having handed the *QE* over to the Americans," wrote de Chair, "we were . . . looking forward to reaching Trinidad the following morning."

The southward leg of the trip took the three destroyers past Florida, the Bahamas, the Dominican Republic, Puerto Rico, and the small Caribbean islands of Montserrat, Dominica, and Saint Lucia. At about six o'clock that night, some forty miles south of Barbados, a watchman on the *Quentin* spotted a torpedo running on the surface spraying water into the air. He sounded a warning, and the captain "maneuvered wildly to evade and did so, but just barely." The *Pathfinder* was the first to make radar contact with the U-boat, and as de Chair put it, "the hunt was on." Each ship dropped underwater bombs called depth charges near the spot where the U-boat had dived. When no wreckage surfaced, it was clear that the U-boat had survived the attack and was still down there, probably lying doggo (as the Brits say, meaning hiding) on the ocean floor. The senior British commander, Edward Gibbs, was on the *Pathfinder*. That ship had the old meter-wavelength radar. So did the *Quentin*. Only the *Vimy* had microwave radar. Gibbs knew the U-boat would eventually have to surface for oxygen. The only question was where. Knowing that the *Vimy*'s radar operator could detect a surfaced U-boat at seven miles, Gibbs ordered de Chair to stay put while the other two ships sailed eastward.

Moonrise that night wasn't until eleven, so the sky, said de Chair, was "pitch dark." Not long after the *Quentin* and *Pathfinder* departed, the *Vimy*'s nineteen-year-old radar operator, Douglas Stott, picked up a blip at twenty-eight hundred yards. The radar reflection told Stott it was a "large surface vessel" moving west. He rushed the report to de Chair, who gave orders to his gunners at the main battery, and they "opened fire from 'A' gun." The second shell slammed into the fuselage of U-162, which up until that moment had been on a three-week ship-sinking spree, sending six merchant ships and three oil tankers to the bottom. Seeing the explosion, de Chair ordered "full speed" toward the U-boat. As the *Vimy* closed in, de Chair turned on the searchlight and saw an American flag painted on the U-boat's conning tower. That was a common ploy, "which did not deceive us," wrote the captain. The

Vimy rammed the U-boat, and British gunners dropped another depth charge. The collision and the resulting explosion caused the U-boat to heel over and start to sink. German sailors, many wearing only black undershorts, climbed out of the hatch and leaped into the waves.

De Chair fired snowflake rocket flares to illuminate the scene. Seeing the bobbing German survivors, *Vimy*'s crewmen threw scramble nets over the side of the ship. Captain de Chair's black cat had sought safety in one of the nets, and it went over the side as well. Hearing a panicked *meow*, a British sailor jumped into the water, rescued the cat, slung it around his neck, and then clambered back up the net alongside the Germans. The soggy crewman was mistaken for a German until he named the cat and its owner.

Forty-eight of fifty Germans who had been onboard U-162 were rescued and taken to Trinidad, where they were herded into a POW (prisoner of war) enclosure and interrogated by British and American officers. One German wanted to know how the *Vimy* had found the U-boat in the dark. He wasn't the only one mystified by improved Allied detection. U-boat captains across the Atlantic had reported it was no longer safe to surface at night. Back in Paris, German U-boat commander Admiral Karl Dönitz concluded that either the Allies had invented "some kind of location device," or a spy had infiltrated U boat command. Unaware of the magnetron or microwave radar, he leaned toward the second explanation and ordered an investigation of every member of his staff. These interrogations yielded names of numerous French girlfriends but no traitors.

Captain de Chair and his crew received a warm welcome in Trinidad. The Americans treated them to ice cream and the latest Hollywood movies. The sailors got haircuts and did their laundry. One went to a dentist to get a rotten tooth pulled, and another celebrated his twentieth birthday with his first sip of the drink "so dear to the heart" of every sailor: rum.

On September 12, *Quentin* and *Pathfinder* departed Trinidad with seven oil tankers bound for Freetown, Sierra Leone.

Four days later, Captain de Chair got his new orders for the *Vimy*: escort five oil tankers across the Atlantic to Gibraltar. The other escort was the HMS *Burdock*, and tagging along with the convoy as far as Barbados was a small Dutch cargo ship, the HNLMS *Prins Willem*. At sunset on September 17, the two escorts and the Dutch ship met the tanker convoy as it emerged from the harbor at Boca di Navios.

On board the *Vimy*, British sailors enjoyed a dinner of honey-baked ham with pineapple slices, mashed potatoes, and stewed red beans. Afterward radar operator Douglas Stott spent four more hours in the radar hut on the upper bridge. No sightings. He was relieved at midnight. The night passed without incident.

The same cannot be said about the night on the raft. Sitting atop the supply chest, Peifer waited for the quarter moon to disappear behind a cloud. Then he stood, eased open the chest, quietly

NO TRESPASSING

Captured U-boat crewmen and officers were sent to Fort Hunt outside Washington, DC. Once questioning was complete, they were transferred to various work camps. Prisoners might have picked potatoes in Maine, cut pulpwood in Virginia, planted cotton in Arizona, or harvested pumpkins in Tennessee. When a crewman from U-162, along with two Germans from other U-boats, escaped from the camp in Crossville, Tennessee, they fled into the nearby woods. Several days later, the trio came to a mountain cabin and started to get water from a pump. "An irascible granny appeared in the doorway, aimed a gun in their direction and told them to 'git.'" The crewmen scoffed and paid no attention. A few moments later, Granny aimed her rifle and fired, killing one of the young men. This old Southern woman must have grown up hearing bloody tales of the Civil War, because she later told a deputy sheriff she fired because, "I thought they wuz Yankees!"

pulled out some chocolate, and ate it. No one saw him. Too dark. But Vargas was awake and smelled the chocolate. So did McDaniel.

The next morning, after whispering to a few others, Vargas said, "Chief, some of us want to talk to you."

"What's up, Vargas?" asked Peifer.

"It's about the food, chief. We want what's left passed out now."

"Why's that, Vargas?"

"Because we don't want nobody left short."

"No more shoplifting after hours," said Rodriguez.

"What makes you say that?" asked the bosun.

"We smelled food last night . . . chocolate," said Vargas, "and we know where it came from."

Peifer didn't deny sneaking the chocolate. Instead he went on the offensive. "You know what'll happen? Some of you damned fools will eat everything you're given all at once."

"That's up to each person to decide," said Greenwell.

"I don't like it," said the bosun.

"You haven't got any choice," replied Vargas.

Peifer sized up his adversaries and said, "Okay, you want the food? You got it! But remember, this is it. No begging for more from somebody else." He motioned to Rodriguez, who opened the food chest and gave everyone two cans of pemmican and the last handfuls of crackers and malted-milk tablets.

"Where's the rest of the food?" someone asked.

"That's it."

"That's all there is!"

"That's all," said Peifer.

"The prospect of receiving any further supply from a plane did not appear too bright," wrote Mrs. Bell.

"Only then did I realize how close to death we were," Robert recalled.

An hour passed. Not a word was spoken.

The *Vimy* had just crossed sixty degrees west longitude. In the radar hut, Douglas Stott picked up a signal. Something was out there.

At this moment—9:50 in the morning on September 18, 1942—radar found the raft.

It was a moment one hundred and fifty years in the making, a moment at the end of a time line that begins with Galvani's frogs and goes on to include Volta's pile, Faraday's magnets, Maxwell's equations, Hertz's spark-gap, Marconi's radio waves, Taylor and Young's transmitter and receiver, Page's duplexer, Watson-Watt's radar towers, Edward Bowen's airborne radar set, and Boot and Randall's cavity magnetron. Also populating the time line are the few "innovation advocates" (such as Dr. Taylor and Rear Admiral Harold Bowen) who sensed the potential of signal detection and wangled the money to fund research, development, and testing.

In another sense, it was a moment just over three years in the making. A World War II time line begins with Hitler's 1939 invasion of Poland and includes the thousands of random, and often lethal, confrontations between people who under normal circumstances would never meet, let alone shoot at or kill, one another. One of these random encounters was about to occur a few hundred miles off the coast of Trinidad. But this one wouldn't be lethal. Or would it?

In the radar hut on the *Vimy*, operator Stott shouted, "Object bearing three hundred and thirty degrees! About five miles."

Stott's partner jotted down the bearing and added the words, "U-boat on the surface."

The message was given to Lieutenant John Craven, a member of the bridge watch.

"I grabbed my binoculars and swept the ocean," recalled Craven. "There it was." He was sure it was the conning tower of a partially submerged U-boat. "I hadn't the slightest doubt," he said.

On the raft, Louis Vega yelled, "Convoy!"

Nobody responded. Too many ships had passed them by to get excited about this one.

"They're coming our way!" shouted Vega.

"How far?"

"Close," said Vega. "Maybe three, four miles."

"How many?"

"Look and see for yourself."

"Never till my dying day shall I forget the sight that greeted me," wrote Mrs. Bell. "There on the horizon . . . was a line of five great merchant ships shepherded by two destroyers of the Allied Nations. The flood of emotion that swept our souls was impossible to describe. We were right in their path, and there did not seem the slightest possibility of their missing us."

On the bridge of the *Vimy*, Lieutenant Craven sent word of the U-boat sighting to Captain de Chair. After peering through his binoculars, he also mistook the raft's little sail for the conning tower of a U-boat. The captain ordered six blasts, a signal that told the other ships not to follow. Turning to Craven, de Chair said, "Attack at all possible speed."

Craven sounded the alarm. The crew raced to action stations. De Chair upped the *Vimy's* speed to nineteen knots and closed in on the target.

Mrs. Bell wrote, "When we saw a destroyer break away and come tearing over the sea towards us, we felt sure we were rescued. On and on she came, the water breaking in great cataracts from her narrow, streamlined bow."

Watching from the bridge, Captain de Chair wondered why the U-boat wasn't diving. Was it damaged? He wasn't worried about torpedoes. They weren't very accurate at this distance, and even if they were, he'd have time to dodge them. What worried him was the U-boat's deck cannon. Forcing the boat to dive eliminated that threat. At three miles he told Craven to open fire.

"Fire A-gun!" shouted Craven. The four-inch cannon roared. "Fire B-gun!" *Ka-boom!*

Shells screamed across the sky at twenty-seven hundred feet per second and exploded all around the raft.

"It was an unbelievable moment of despair," Mary recalled. Mrs. Bell wrote, "All our hard experiences of the past three weeks seemed to culminate in this last terror. One shell burst a short distance ahead of us, casting up an enormous cataract of yellowish-green water. Another struck the water and ricocheted over our heads." Flying metal shards ripped through the sail and cut down the mast. "Oh God, not now! Not this way!" shouted McDaniel. The children "screamed in terror," wrote Mrs. Bell, and threw themselves "down in the bottom of the raft." She and several crewmen piled on top of them.

But not Peifer. Despite the incoming shells and the geysers of water erupting fore and aft, the bosun stood tall, grabbed the shattered mast, and started waving the torn sail from side to side. The bossy bully had turned into a death-defying savior.

Peering through his binoculars, Captain de Chair thought it was strange when the U-boat's "upper works" suddenly disappeared, and he saw someone waving "a dirty white flag." He gave orders to cease fire and reduce speed. As they got closer, de Chair realized that "the object looked rather too small for a conning tower." Not until the *Vimy* got within a mile did de Chair realize what his gunners had been shelling. "People packed tight together, standing on a raft whose sail we had shot away." Miraculously that was the only damage.

"As we drew alongside, this ragged party made a brave but pathetic sight," wrote de Chair.

"Who are you?" a British sailor shouted.

"We're Americans!" Peifer shouted.

"We're survivors from a torpedoed ship."

"You sons of bitches. . . . you coulda killed us!" yelled a crewman.

"Come on, laddie. You're all right now," replied a Scotsman on the ship.

Mary wrote that the clean-shaven young men lining the rail of the *Vimy* were the most "wonderful sight" she'd ever seen. Over sixty years later she wrote, "I still get goose bumps" about that moment.

This time the sailors made sure Captain de Chair's black cat wasn't snoozing in the scramble net before they heaved it over the side. On the *Vimy*, an officer named Raymond Venables "ran for a machine gun and sprayed bullets" at the circling sharks. Venables said that normally he wouldn't shoot creatures "just being themselves," but this was not a normal situation.

Peifer was the only one of the seventeen rafters still strong enough to climb up the nets by himself. "He seemed surprisingly fit," said Stott.

"Hands reached down to pull me up," wrote Mary. "As soon as my feet touched the deck, a sailor lifted me in his arms and carried me below deck. It was unbelievable to sit on red leather seats in the captain's lounge—just past unbelievable." Venables carried Carol Shaw up the netting and remembered that her first comment was, "I'm glad you picked us up." The two of them would reminisce about that moment when they spoke by phone twelve years later.

Mrs. Bell broke a rib when she toppled over the rail and onto the deck of the *Vimy*, but she wouldn't let that ache interfere with her joy at being rescued. She too was carried to the captain's lounge, and remembered the "big, comfortable armchair where I could rest my back." Messmen brought bread, bowls of hot tomato soup, apples, and oranges. George Marano recalled "that those Brits gave us their day's supply of rum." Doctors arrived with washbasins and bandages, and later sailors distributed navy outfits to the guys, while Mrs.

Bell, Mary, and Carol were given dresses that some of the more adventuresome sailors had worn to a costume party in Trinidad.

After a few hours of sleep, the survivors were awakened for a transfer to the Dutch ship that was about to leave the convoy and head for Barbados. "The British were so good to us," said Robert, "the last thing we wanted to do was leave the *Vimy*." But Captain de Chair had orders to get those oil tankers to Gibraltar.

Carol Shaw in the arms of Sub Lieutenant Raymond Venables on board HMS Vimy

Even with ocean swells of only two to three feet, the transfer was tricky business. Rope lines were tossed from one ship to another, and when the two vessels bumped, the captain of the *Prins Willem* let loose with some Dutch words that are best not translated. The survivors were hoisted into slings that slid across the ropes. "Our last view of the destroyer," wrote Mrs. Bell, "was of the captain and the officers watching from the bridge, and the sailors crowding the deck, all waving farewell and calling out their good wishes."

The Dutch sailors were just as hospitable as the Brits. The steward brought Mrs. Bell a cup of tea while the children were treated to thick slices of warm bread covered with strawberry jam.

Each person was given a bunk, but most were too excited to sleep. It was late afternoon when the throb of the engines ceased, and the ship's whistle blew. Robert peered out a porthole and saw the lights and buildings of Bridgetown, capital of Barbados, then a British colony. With its red-tiled roofs and coral-white streets, the port town was postcard-worthy. But underneath the tropical beauty was this sad truth: the war had crippled the Barbadian economy. Demand for sugar, its main export, had plummeted. People were jobless and hungry. Added to this misery was a steady stream of survivors from U-boat attacks. Government officials could have closed their harbor and sent the hundreds of U-boat victims to nearby Martinique or Saint Vincent. But they didn't. All who made it to Bridgetown were welcomed.

Open motorboats transported the rafters from the ship to the docks where members of the St. John's Ambulance Brigade were waiting with stretchers. Joe Greenwell insisted on walking. "I remember taking two or three steps," he said. "Then I fell flat on the ground."

Ambulances drove the rafters to the general hospital. The driver told Mary that he had seen many survivors of U-boat attacks, but all were young men in lifeboats. "We were the first from a raft," he said, and were "the longest at sea and the only [group] with a woman and children." Mrs. Bell recalled the joy of listening to the noises of a town: "the laughter of men and women, the cry of little children playing in the streets, and the hundred and one other noises that we all take as a matter of course in our daily lives, but which now . . . told us that our nightmare was ended."

The doctors and nurses were amazed how few of the rafters were sunburned. People found on lifeboats or rafts often had sun poisoning. It was the palm oil that protected them, just as Captain Bogdan had said it would. The bad news for Mrs. Bell was that the oil had cemented her hair into one big knot. The only solution was to cut it all off.

September 20 was Mary's fourteenth birthday. The nurses asked her if she wanted anything special. "I decided I would like cream puffs," she said. "I had never tasted one, but a missionary girl in Ivory Coast [used to eat them]." So "we all had cream puffs for my birthday."

Most of the rafters were able to walk after three days. When given permission to stroll about the hospital, many crewmen sought out Mrs. Bell to thank her for all her prayers. Greenwell said, "Her being [on the raft] had a great effect on the rest of us, helping us to keep our heads, preventing us from doing things that might have been the end of us all." Potter presented Mrs. Bell with a gift: his jackknife. Louis Vega hugged her and later told an interviewer, "She saved my life, by God. . . . She made the rain come."

Peifer didn't visit. Interviewed after the rescue, the bosun told a reporter from the *Barbados Advocate* that "God helps those who help themselves," and while on the raft he was determined to help himself. The reporter called Peifer "the hero of the story," and a month later, the merchant marines awarded Peifer the bronze medal for valor. The citation included a quote from *Vimy's* Captain de Chair, who said that Bosun Peifer "deserves great credit for the fine spirit and fettle in which his raft crew was found when picked up."

Robert Bell and Richard Shaw were released from the hospital after five days, and a local church placed them both with a family who lived in a spacious hillside home overlooking the harbor. Richard said he gained seven pounds in one week, and Robert gained ten. Mary Bell spent seven days in the hospital and then went to stay with a different family.

Mrs. Bell, who was suffering from exhaustion and her broken rib, needed three weeks to recover. Carol Shaw also remained in the hospital so her fractured elbow (now set and casted) could heal. Doctors said that "there was every prospect that the bone would knit perfectly." Carol was a "brave little soldier," said Mrs. Bell.

The hospital bill in Barbados for all three Bells came to $150, roughly one-fifth of what it might have been in Boston or New York. All their medical and travel expenses were paid for by the central office of the Christian and Missionary Alliance. Expenses for Richard and Carol Shaw were covered by their parents' sponsoring agency, Baptist Mid-Missions in Mishawaka, Indiana.

From Barbados, the Bells and the Shaw children flew to the American base in Trinidad. There the US Navy helped Mrs. Bell secure five seats on a flight to Miami, where a representative from Baptist Mid-Missions met the Shaw children and escorted them by train to the Missionary Children's Home and school in Batesburg, South Carolina. Richard said he was glad to have his sister with him. "I didn't used to think much of my sister," he wrote, "but now I do." Both Shaw children were eventually adopted: Carol by a family in Detroit, Michigan, and Richard by an aunt in Burlington, Iowa.

Following a two-day layover in Miami, the Bells flew to LaGuardia Airport in New York. Finally, on October 23, Robert, Mary, and Ethel Bell walked through the front door of their house in Nyack. That night they slept in their own beds for the first time in four years.

The next day Mrs. Bell received a call from a government official who asked her to travel to Washington, DC, for an "official debriefing by various government agencies." She spent a day giving a firsthand account of the U-boat attack, the aftermath, the three weeks at sea, the harrowing final moments on the raft, and the rescue. When those meetings ended, Mrs. Bell returned home, and she and the children took the train to Toronto, Canada, for a joyous reunion with Mrs. Bell's parents. On Halloween Robert and Mary went trick-or-treating with their grandpa. Even he wore a costume.

The Bells' trip to Canada coincided with a major development in the radar world. A new United States Antisubmarine Command was established, and its opening move was outfitting two hundred long-range B-24 bombers with mass-produced air-to-surface-vessel microwave radar. The model of radar—the SCR-517—had been "rushed into production to meet the mounting U-boat peril." Aircraft so equipped could patrol three thousand square miles of ocean in an hour, tripling the area that could be scanned with the old meter-wave radar. As soon as English Prime Minister Winston Churchill heard about this upgrade, he wrote to President Roosevelt asking for thirty such planes to confront "the U-boat menace," which he called "our worst danger." Roosevelt met Churchill more than halfway, sending him twenty-one of the new planes, which the British Royal Air Force called Liberators. By May 1943, a combined allied force of 230 Liberators, along with a fleet of microwave-equipped war ships, had sunk 25 percent of the German U-boat fleet in the Atlantic. In May alone, the Allies sank 38 U-boats.

German U-boat Commander Karl Dönitz confessed to Hitler that with their new location devices, Allied planes "can carry out surprise attacks [even] when the ceiling is low, visibility poor, or at night." The "losses are too high," Dönitz reported, and it was impossible to know if "submarine warfare will again become effective." Hitler worried that this "new detection device might involve [scientific] principles with which we are not familiar." Dönitz agreed. "We don't ... know on what wave length the enemy locates us." In a radio address to the German people, Hitler said, "the temporary setback to our U-boat campaign is due to one single technical invention of our enemies." The setback, it turned out, wasn't temporary. In August 1943, Dönitz ordered all U-boats in the Atlantic and the Caribbean to return to their French bases. That summer, 3,546 Allied cargo ships, troop transports, and oil tankers made the crossing from the United States to Britain. Not one was torpedoed.

Microwave radar had rewritten the rules of warfare, and the Allies had won the two-year-long Battle of the Atlantic. From that point on, military experts knew that "although far from defeated, [the Axis countries] could not win the war."

CHAPTER 14
RECONCILIATION

ON SEPTEMBER 23, 1942, twenty-five days after the *West Lashaway* sank, one of the other three rafts washed ashore on the southeast beach of Saint Vincent in the Caribbean. There were only two men aboard. Navy Gunner's Mate Dalton Munn died on the way to the hospital. Able Seaman Elliott Gurney survived. Inside the raft's supply chest, Allied naval authorities found "an envelope containing an American Express money order and a certified check. Both were payable to Mr. Harvey Shaw." Gurney confirmed that Mr. Shaw had been on that raft but had died. "The missionary [man] taught us to pray," he said. The two other rafts were never found. Of the fifty-six people who'd sailed from Takoradi on the *West Lashaway* on August 15, forty-two survived the torpedo attack. But only eighteen lived to tell the story—seventeen of whom were on one raft.

In August 1943, Mrs. Bell gave an interview to a writer for *Good Housekeeping* magazine, which reached over 2.5 million homes. The resulting article began with the words: "Here, readers, is one of the great stories of faith. It is a true story. It happened." Eager to make the most of Mrs. Bell's sudden fame, the Christian and Missionary Alliance sent her on a speaking tour throughout the United States and Canada. In churches and meeting halls in cities, towns, and villages, Mrs. Bell recounted the sinking-and-survival story, always concluding with the thought that "God had spared her life and the lives of her children for a purpose," and that she was determined to spend her remaining years "so conformed to His will that the plan and purpose He has for me and for my children may be gloriously fulfilled."

During the first few months of Mrs. Bell's lecture tour, Mary and Robert stayed with their grandparents in Toronto. When it became clear that the tour would extend through 1944, Mrs. Bell took Mary and Robert to South Carolina and enrolled them in the same boarding school that Carol and Richard Shaw had briefly attended three years earlier. Not until 1945 did all three Bells return to their home in New York.

There Mary attended Nyack High School, where she reconnected with old friends from fifth grade. After graduating in 1947, Mary headed off to Nyack College. Two years later, Robert followed. With both children out of the house, the woman *Good Housekeeping* magazine referred to as "gentle little Ethel Bell" sailed off yet again for the Ivory Coast, where she would continue her religious work and start a school for girls in the town of Béoumi, just sixty miles west of her earlier post in Bouaké. Sadly, Mrs. Bell's demanding schedule prevented her from traveling home to attend Mary's 1950 wedding to her college boyfriend, Elmer Whitbeck (a former marine). The newlyweds spent several years doing missionary work in the Badlands of South Dakota before moving to Lincoln, Nebraska, where Elmer joined the staff of the radio broadcast *Back to the Bible*. The Whitbecks eventually raised five children.

Robert also graduated from Nyack College. He went on to earn a master's degree in education at the State University of New York at New Paltz, and then did postgraduate studies at Hofstra University in Hempstead, New York. For thirty-four years he worked as a fourth-grade teacher and later as a principal in the Three Village School District on Long Island, New York.

For two decades after the war, except for an annual recounting of the raft story for his students, Robert rarely spoke about the experience. He had little desire to relive those grim days and weeks. But beginning in the mid-1960s, Robert began receiving invitations to share his story with various local civic and religious groups. At many of these engagements, audience members asked questions Robert couldn't answer.

At a banquet in 1975, one person asked Robert if he had a picture of the *West Lashaway*. When Robert said he didn't, the audience member suggested he write to the Mariners' Museum in Newport News, Virginia. "That was the first step," said Robert, "toward my acquiring a half-dozen scrapbooks of photos, documents, and correspondence from anyone and everyone who could possibly offer me information about our story and its details."

Among the experts he contacted was Dean Allard, the director of naval history at the National Archives in Washington, DC. Allard gave Robert the name and address of Dr. Jürgen Rohwer, a U-boat expert at the Bibliothek für Zeitgeschichte (Library of Contemporary History) in Stuttgart, West Germany. Robert connected with Dr. Rohwer, who was able to use the date and location of *West Lashaway*'s sinking to determine that the ship had been torpedoed by U-66, captained by Friedrich Markworth. Rohwer told Robert that Captain Markworth and several U-66 crew members were still alive, and he passed along their mailing addresses.

In spring 1978 Robert posted several letters. He was reaching out to the former U-boaters, he said, because he had "great curiosity about events surrounding my experience." In the last paragraph of the letters, Robert assured the Germans that he had "no vindictive motive." He understood that "each side of the war was doing its duty, and all that is over." Robert said later he had "no clear expectation that my letters would be well received or answered."

Not only were they well received *and* answered, they led to a three-year-long correspondence. Captain Markworth wrote, "I am happy that you were able to survive this horrible episode in your life." One of the German crewmen wrote, "I am very sorry that you, as a child, had to suffer such a terrible time." Another wrote, "Often, after the war, I thought about what happened to those who survived the ships which we torpedoed. Therefore, I was very happy to hear that some managed to reach a harbor or were saved."

As it turned out, these German sailors knew well what Robert had been through. On the night of May 5–6, 1944, about four hundred miles west of the Cape Verde Islands, U-66 was sunk by a US destroyer, the *Buckley*. Thirty-six German sailors survived, but twenty-four did not.

On September 25, 1981, Robert and his wife, Ruth, boarded a Lufthansa airliner and flew from New York to Düsseldorf, West Germany, where they were the guests of honor at a small U-66–*West Lashaway* reunion. Just before the meal, Georg Olschewski, the seventy-two-year-old former lead engineer on U-66, tapped on his glass, waited for quiet, and said, "Mr. Bell . . . fortunately now we are friends and forget the former enmity; we hope we will be friends forever. I don't want to make a big political talk. We only want you to know how glad we are that you made the long trip to see us." He reached for a metal commemorative plate and handed it to Robert. "Please take this plate, which is given by the crew of U-66 as a memento." On it was the insignia of the Second U-Boat Flotilla and U-66. "I hope you will hold us in good memory."

The following year Robert and Ruth welcomed the U-66 radioman Karl Degener-Böning and his wife, Hilde, into their home. Mary Bell Whitbeck flew in, as did eighty-three-year-old Joe Greenwell (with whom Robert had reconnected in 1979).

Robert said he recognized in Degener-Böning "a man deeply moved by and sensitive to the hardships endured by those who had suffered because of submarine attacks." It's a sad truth of history, Robert wrote later, that "the hostility of nations makes needless enemies of otherwise decent men."

Four years later, Robert arranged one last (and slightly different) reunion in Frankfurt, Germany. This one included not just survivors of U-66, but also the commander of the *Buckley*, Brent Abel, who rescued as many Germans as he could after sinking U-66.

Being as close to a clergyman as anyone that day, Robert was asked to say grace. After the meal, when it came time for speeches, Captain Abel concluded his remarks by saying, "I am now seventy-one years old. In my entire life, there is no accomplishment of which I am as proud as that the USS *Buckley* under my direction took the risks and made the choices that enabled us to save the lives of those of you and your shipmates who survived. I wish we could have saved more. I know my shipmates, whether here or not, agree."

The U-66 radioman Karl Degener-Böning rose, thanked the Americans for traveling so far "to shake hands with us," and called the evening "a highlight of our lives."

Robert Bell flew home the next day because the school year in Stony Brook had just started. He took with him another commemorative plate. This one said, "Enemies Become Friends."

MARINE MARAUDER

Reinhard Hardegen was a U-boat captain. On the night of January 15, 1942, he guided U-123 into the waters twenty-five miles east of New York City. He had no detailed nautical charts, no sailing directions, no list of light signals. "The war with America came on so suddenly and unexpectedly," he wrote, that U-boat command "had no operational charts or other materials for that part of the world." All Hardegen had were guidebooks from a French municipal library. He surfaced south of Rockaway Beach and let the coastal lights from Long Island guide him westward. As he approached the silver glow of Manhattan and its neighboring boroughs, he said the moment was "unbelievably beautiful and great . . . for the first time in this war, a German soldier looked out on the east coast of the U.S.A." In 1999, Hardegen told an interviewer, "I was not a Nazi. I did my duty for my country, not for Hitler." Hardegen was the last surviving U-boat captain. He died in Bremen, Germany, in June 2018. He was 105 years old.

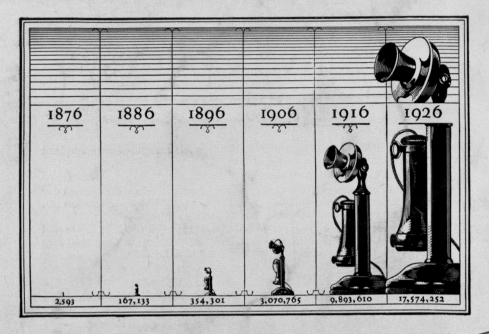

1876	1886	1896	1906	1916	1926
2,593	167,133	354,301	3,070,765	9,893,610	17,574,252

Milestones in National Service

An Advertisement of
the American Telephone and Telegraph Company

THERE are twenty-five Bell companies but only one Bell System —and one Bell aim and ideal, stated by President Walter S. Gifford as:

"A telephone service for this nation, so far as humanly possible free from imperfections, errors or delays, and enabling anyone anywhere at any time to pick up a telephone and talk to anyone else anywhere else in this country, clearly, quickly and at a reasonable cost."

The past year brought the service of the Bell Telephone System measurably nearer that goal. Seven hundred and eighty-one thousand telephones were added to the System—bringing the total number interconnected in and with the Bell to more than

seventeen and a half million. The number of applications waiting for service, including those in new and outlying sections, was reduced fifty per cent.

A third transcontinental telephone line was completed to the Pacific coast. The largest number of miles of toll wire for one year was added to the system—more than 600,000 miles. The average length of time for completing toll calls throughout the System was lowered by thirty-five seconds.

A seven per cent improvement over the previous year was made in the quality of voice transmission in toll calls.

An adjustment was made in long distance rates amounting to a reduction of about $3,000,000 annually.

An old phone advertisement, overlaid with drawings of different phones over the years

CHAPTER 15
EIGHT DECADES OF RADAR

ON APRIL 30, 1945, with well-supplied Allied armies closing in on the German capital of Berlin, Adolf Hitler died by suicide. A week later, Germany surrendered. Italy had already surrendered two years earlier, following the Battle of the Atlantic. Japan kept fighting until August 15, 1945, when they became the last of the Axis countries to lay down their arms. As in World War I, it was American military and manufacturing power that propelled the Allies to victory. When the fighting ended, much of that manufacturing was channeled into developing and producing new and profitable devices for peacetime use.

On ocean liners, cargo ships, and yachts, radar provided insurance against collisions with icebergs, rocky coastlines, and other ships. In the air, radar alerted pilots to the presence of mountain peaks, skyscrapers, and nearby aircraft.

The same year the war ended, a self-taught American engineer named Percy Spencer was working on an active radar set in a lab at the Raytheon Corporation just outside Boston. At some point he became aware that the candy bar in his pocket was melting. *Hmmm.* Were microwaves generating the heat? Spencer cleaned the mess out of his pocket and placed some popcorn kernels near the radar set. When they began popping, Spencer realized that microwaves could heat food. Raytheon filed a patent, and two years later Spencer and his colleagues unveiled the world's first microwave oven. It was called the Radarange, and it was as large as a refrigerator and weighed more than seven hundred pounds. A Boston restaurant agreed to use it for test purposes. By 1954 Raytheon scientists had figured out how to reduce the size of the microwave oven, and the company introduced the first home-kitchen version, which sold for two thousand dollars (about sixteen thousand dollars in today's money). Over the next three decades, the price of microwave ovens kept dropping, and sales kept increasing. By the time George H. W. Bush was elected president in 1988, customers were buying a million units a year at a price of $250 each. Today you can buy a microwave oven for as little as $50.

In April 1947 at National Airport (now called Ronald Reagan Washington National) in Washington, DC, technicians began testing a radar system called ground-controlled approach (GCA), which allowed air traffic controllers on the ground to guide pilots to runways. The system utilized two radar antennas with narrow "pencil beams." One beam scanned side to side, the other up and down. President Harry Truman became the first chief executive to land in a plane guided by GCA.

UNINTENDED CONSEQUENCES

After the war, Robert Watson-Watt spent time living and working in Canada. One day, as he and his wife, Jean, drove from Toronto to Kingston, Ontario, Robert heard "a police bell" and pulled over his Buick Century. The policeman charged him with speeding. "How did you do it?" asked Watson-Watt. "Was it by radar?" The policeman said his detection device was an "electronic speed-meter," and he wasn't sure how it worked. Jean leaned over and said to the policeman, "You may be interested to know that King George VI knighted my husband for inventing radar." The policeman wasn't impressed and ordered Watson-Watt to pay the $12.50 fine for "driving at an excessive speed." As he handed over the money, Watson-Watt said, "Had I known what you were going to do with [radar], I would never have invented it!"

In 1951 microwave technology was used to transmit America's first national live television broadcast, and four years later, a Zenith Electronics Corporation engineer named Eugene Polley invented the wireless remote. He called it a Flashmatic, and it worked by transmitting electromagnetic waves from the small device to a receiver inside the TV. By the 1980s, remotes were slipping between sofa cushions in houses from Maine to California.

In 1959 the National Weather Service established its first network of radars dedicated to warning people about severe weather.

The 1970s saw a flurry of new uses for radar. In 1972, it was used to track insect migrations, and the following year, Chicago-based engineer Martin Cooper used radio wave technology to invent the first hand-held cellular phone. Called the Motorola DynaTAC 8000X, it was ten inches long, weighed two-and-a-half pounds, and lasted twenty-five minutes on a charge. When the first mobile cell phones went on sale, the price was $3,995.

In March 1975, when baseball players traveled south for spring training, the pitchers were introduced to a radar gun that measured the speed of their fast balls. It was a Michigan State University baseball coach named Danny Litwhiler who first came up with the

A radar gun like those used by police officers to record the speed of passing cars

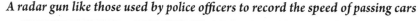

idea to model a baseball radar gun after the device police officers had been using (since 1947) to nab drivers exceeding speed limits.

In 1977 the first MRI (magnetic resonance imaging) exam was performed on a live human. It's a painless procedure—the patient lies in a tube-like machine that uses electromagnetic waves and a strong magnetic field to produce detailed three-dimensional images of the inside of the body. It's lifesaving technology.

The keyless fob used to lock and unlock car doors was invented in 1982 by a Frenchman named Paul Lipschultz, who worked for automaker Renault. The company took the *P* from Paul and the *lip* from his surname, and called the device a plipper. Key fobs work by transmitting electromagnetic waves to a receiver in the car.

In 1983 the US Navy made its global positioning system available to the public. GPS is made up of radar transmitting stations, receivers, and at least thirty-one orbiting satellites. Today when you use a smartphone to determine your location, you get information from at least four of those satellites.

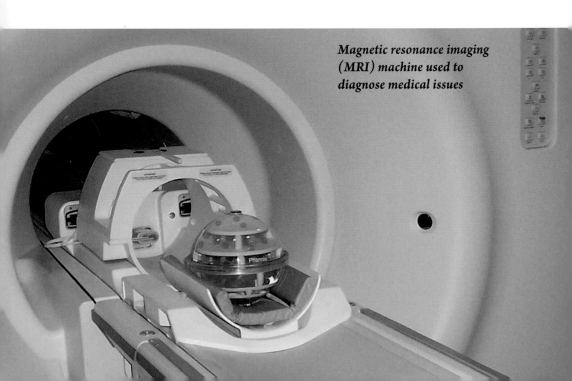

Magnetic resonance imaging (MRI) machine used to diagnose medical issues

By 1990 a new radar system at John F. Kennedy Airport in New York made it possible for forty-nine planes to land each hour on parallel runways, no matter the weather.

In 1992 radio waves were used to send the first text message, and American and French scientists began using a radar-equipped satellite to monitor sea-level rise, a key indicator of climate change.

In 1994 the General Motors Corporation introduced a car radar system "that warns drivers if they are about to hit another car when changing lanes."

Tesla Corporation released its first electric car, called the Roadster, in 2008. The electricity was generated using the same method Faraday used: by varying the magnetic field.

In 2014 scientists got their most detailed look at the moon's surface after signals beamed from a radar dish in Puerto Rico bounced off the moon and reflected to a radio telescope in West Virginia.

In 2019 Google released the first smartphone with a radar-powered sensor. The Pixel 4 phone allowed a hands-free user to control the phone with gestures.

In December 2022, American and French climate scientists sent a newly improved sea-level monitoring satellite into orbit that promised greater resolution than the older one. With the new technology, scientists were able to confirm that, due to rising temperatures and melting ice caps, the South Atlantic has risen six-and-a-half inches since the Bells and their fellow rafters floated over those ocean swells during that long ago summer of 1942.

Today radar technology is the vital component in things that once seemed unimaginable: driverless cars, drone deliveries, smart watches, artificial intelligence, mapping outer space, human health monitoring, and electronic warfare. Who knows what electromagnetic "dream stuff" will be the reality of tomorrow?

EPILOGUE

EXCEPT FOR FURLOUGHS in 1954 and 1958, Mrs. Bell served in West Africa until 1962, when she retired at age sixty-nine. Back in the United States, she spent the next sixteen years living in villages for elderly missionaries—one in Glendale, California, the other in Deland, Florida. In 1978, unable to care for herself, she moved in with Mary. Mrs. Bell died in 1983 at age ninety.

Mary Bell Whitbeck spent her final years in Sterling and Tecumseh, Nebraska. The teenage girl who thought she was going to drown in August 1942 lived until 2019. Like her mother, she made it to age ninety. She had sixteen grandchildren and "a multitude of great-grandchildren."

Robert Bell retired in 1992 and moved to Sarasota, Florida. Before he died in 2014, he was grandfather to five grandchildren, and it's likely there were many nights when one or more of the little ones begged their grandpa to tell them (yet again) the raft story.

Having tracked down Douglas Stott, the *Vimy* radar operator, Robert knew the role that microwave radar played in his rescue. Living into the twenty-first century meant he could appreciate how seamlessly microwave technology had been woven into the fabric of his life and the lives of his two daughters and grandkids. It's easy to imagine Robert, at his story's end, urging his grandkids to give an occasional thought to how all that "magic" happens and to think about how we owe much of our comfort, safety, and even our liberty to the scientists and engineers who, as Michael Faraday said, "looked into these things and ascertained the very beautiful laws and conditions by which we . . . live and stand upon the earth."

Oh, and one more thing. The fifty million dollars of Congolese gold is still twelve thousand feet deep in the Atlantic. Joe Greenwell said that when navy men interrogated him in the Barbados hospital, he never mentioned the gold. "As far as I was concerned," he said, "that secret belonged to Captain Bogdan and me."

In 2016 shipwreck hunter Gene Birdsong posted the following notice online: "An expedition is being assembled at this time to locate and salvage this ship [the *West Lashaway*]. Please contact me directly at [email address]."

One respondent commented: "Good luck Gene, sounds like a hugely expensive operation, make it pay." Alas, Mr. Birdsong died in 2017 before making the search. No new expeditions have been announced.

ACKNOWLEDGMENTS

THANKS to my incisive and decisive editor, Karen Boss, who once again has worked her editorial alchemy, turning several sprawling and rudderless early drafts into the book you hold in your hands. Karen's ability to immediately perceive the spine of the story and then to guide me through draft after draft makes her an indispensable collaborator. Maya Myers, ace copyeditor, saved me from misspellings, dangling participles, and the passive voice. And executive editor Alyssa Mito Pusey educated me on the difference between sushi and sashimi. Thanks to designer Diane Earley for making the book a work of art, and thanks to Donna Spurlock and her team for promoting the book far and wide.

Another huge thank-you to Alan Hirshfeld, professor of astrophysics at the University of Massachusetts Dartmouth. Author of a wise and witty biography about Michael Faraday, he was kind enough to spend several hours marking up an early draft and explaining the difference between Archimedes's Law of Buoyancy and Newton's Third Law of Motion.

Thanks also to professors Jack Fineberg at the University of Southern California, Adam Cohen at Harvard, Lawrence Principe at Johns Hopkins, David Bercuson at the University of Calgary, James Stigler and Karen Givven at UCLA, and Roald Hoffman at

Cornell. My email exchange with Professor Hoffman is my first with a Nobel Prize winner.

Many librarians and archivists helped guide me through the primary and secondary material. Many thanks to Nathaniel Patch and Alicia Henneberry at the National Archives in College Park, Maryland; Loma Karklins at Caltech; Edith Sandler and Chamisa Redmond at the Library of Congress; Adam Minakowski at the US Naval Academy; Clive Kidd at the Collingwood Heritage Collection; Belinda Haley at the research room at the Imperial War Museum; Sandra Fox at the Washington Navy Yard; and Tobias Thelen at the Bibliothek für Zeitgeschichte in Stuttgart, Germany. And thanks to the whole team at the cozy, cool, and quiet National Archive in Waltham, Massachusetts, including Joan Gearin, Andrew Begley, Daniel Fleming, Joe Keefe, Tracy Skrabut, and Nathaniel Wiltzen.

For patiently answering my questions about elementary physics, I thank my cousin Dr. Richard Oppenheim (of Bell Laboratory) and two of my former fifth-grade students, Jacob and Zach Witten. For guidance on dissection, thanks to neurologist Dr. Michael Stanley at Massachusetts General Hospital. For much-needed digital help tracking down bookworthy images, thanks to my nephew Julian Kafka.

Thanks to my savvy manager, Steven Rosen, and to writer and historian Jonathan Dimbleby, whose 2016 book, *The Battle of the Atlantic*, inspired me to dig deeper into both the battle and the development of radar.

Finally, thanks to LeeAn for everything else.

SOURCE NOTES

Please see the bibliography on pages 177–181 for more information about the cited works. I've also included some juicy historical tidbits that I was unable to shoehorn into the narrative.

Historians, like miners, do a lot of digging. The ore historians seek is not gold or silver, but rather primary source documents. While researching the Battle of the Atlantic, I hit a mother lode when I found not one, not two, but *five* first-person accounts of the sinking of the *West Lashaway* and the twenty days on the raft. For this eyewitness testimony, I thank Ethel, Robert, and Mary Bell, and Richard and Carol Shaw. The details, descriptions, and dialogue they remembered inform so much of this book.

One note: In both editions of the Bell and Lockerbie book, the authors changed the name of Bosun James Peifer to James Owen. But no James Owen appears on any official crew lists. Nor is the bosun identified as such in newspaper reports or in other first-person accounts. No explanation is offered for the name change.

EPIGRAPHS
p. vi: "Any sufficiently . . . from magic": Clarke, p. 39.
p. vi: "I shall pray . . . in God": Fisher, p. 10.
p. vi: "Hell is . . . crowded raft": Bell and Lockerbie (1984), p. 90.

PROLOGUE
p. 2: "radio . . . and ranging": Buderi, p. 56. The US Navy officers credited with coining the name *radar* were Lieutenant Commanders Samuel M. Tucker and F. R. Furth. The new word was adopted by the US military in 1940. Radar historian Louis Brown wrote that the British began using the word in July 1943. As for the Australians, wrote Brown, they "have their own way with language and called the new device a 'doover'" (Brown, L., p. 83).
p. 2, sidebar: In 1942 . . . returning to port: Paone.

p. 3: Knowing where . . . to victory: Tzu. Sun Tzu wrote that "foreknowledge" is what enables "the good general to strike and conquer, and achieve things beyond the reach of ordinary men."
p. 3: Indeed the scientists . . . World War II: Brown, I.., p. 463. For example, British physicist John Randall wrote in 1946, "If we are asked the question—'What scientific development contributed most to the winning of the war?'—we should all undoubtedly answer 'Radar.' . . . [It] helped us to stave off the enemy at a critical time, and carried us to victory in Europe" (Randall, 303). Physics and chemistry professor David Fisher wrote in 1986, "Taken all in all, radar must be the most important scientific/political/military invention of them all, bar none" (Fisher, D., p. xi).

CHAPTER 1: OFF TO AFRICA

p. 5: "Daddy! . . . gone to heaven'": Bell and Lockerbie (1984), p. 74.

p. 6: "loving father" and "fair but firm": ibid., p. 75.

p. 6: "Be not dismayed . . . help thee": ibid.

p. 6: Ivory Coast . . . also spoken: My imagined guidebook entry draws from several online sources including: Palmer; StudyCountry.com; Wikipedia "Ivory Coast"; Comhaire.

p. 8: The nearest . . . of Guinea: Bell and Lockerbie (1984), p. 76.

p. 9: After their classes . . . league baseball: ibid., p. 198. Major league baseball remained segregated until April 10, 1947, when the Brooklyn Dodgers signed Jackie Robinson. Five days later, Robinson became the first Black player to take the field in a major league game.

p. 9, sidebar: Four years later . . . rescued: Blair, *Hunted*, p. 65.

p. 11: At the same . . . European war: Spirit of St. Louis 2 Project. In the late 1930s and early 1940s, Charles Lindbergh crisscrossed the country arguing against American intervention in the war. September 11, 1941, found Lindbergh in Des Moines, Iowa. "Men and women of Iowa," he told the cheering crowd, "We are on the verge of a war for which we are still unprepared, and for which no one has offered a feasible plan for victory—a war which cannot be won without sending our soldiers across the ocean to force a landing on a hostile coast against armies stronger than our own. We are on the verge of war, but it is not yet too late to stay out. It is not too late to show that no amount of money, or propaganda, or patronage can force a free and independent people into war against its will." Joseph Kennedy, the American ambassador to Great Britain, echoed similar thoughts when he spoke in London on March 19, 1938. "It must be realized that the great majority of Americans oppose any entangling alliances" (Kuhn). Two years later, Kennedy told a reporter, "I'm willing to spend all I've got left to keep us out of the war" (Lyons).

p. 11: "war message" and "delay . . . danger": University of Virginia Miller Center.

p. 11: Congress didn't delay . . . in the house: Turner.

p. 12: "There were many . . . those days": Bell, E., p. 16.

p. 12, sidebar: "was the . . . a range": Brown, L., p. 218.

CHAPTER 2: ESCAPE

p. 16: "was the beginning . . . super adventure": Whitbeck, "Rainbow," p. 1.

p. 16: "From 'Bobo' . . . Ouagadougou": ibid., p. 2.

p. 16: "We left . . . helping us": ibid.

p. 17: "What a relief . . . our journey": Bell, E., p. 17.

p. 17: "They not only . . . Gulf of Guinea: El-Akkad.

p. 17: "Mother found . . . and peas": Bell and Lockerbie (1984), p. 110.

p. 18: "Everything was tied . . . effort": ibid., p. 108.

p. 18: "Mary and I . . . Accra": ibid.

p. 19: Every street . . . a gramophone: Plageman, p. 105.

p. 19: a block-long maze . . . size and color: Wikipedia, "Makola Market."

p. 20: "I could . . . Accra forever": Bell and Lockerbie (1984), p. 110.

p. 20: A German plane . . . of Chad: Wikipedia, "*Sonderkommando Blaich*."

p. 20: every night . . . into Gold Coast: Burman. Burman wrote that the propaganda-spouting announcer imitated the "other trained parrots of the Hitler aviary."

p. 21: "stroll around the streets of Accra": Bell and Lockerbie (1984), p. 108.

p. 21, sidebar: "wads of money": Plageman, p. 105.

CHAPTER 3: CURRENT EVENTS

p. 23: According to . . . frog soup: Whittaker, p. 70.

p. 24: "animal electricity," and "inherent in the animal itself": ibid.

p. 24: "These [tingling] sensations . . . was maintained": Dibner, p. 126.

p. 25: "incessantly and without intermission" and "natural electric organ": ibid., p. 112.

p. 25: "detailed anatomical studies": Wu, p. 606.

p. 25: "a succession . . . a weak condition" and "could be . . . of recuperation": Royal Society of Publishing, p. 27.

p. 26: "the singular property . . . its operations": Royal Society of Publishing, p. 27.

p. 26: Volta reported . . . electric circuit: Tretkoff.

p. 26: "voltaic pile": Gregersen.

p. 27: He knew that . . . with electricity: National Archives, "Benjamin Franklin." As early as 1752, Benjamin Franklin wrote to James Bowdoin about "Communication of Magnetism to Needles by Electricity."

p. 27: "but some . . . before the lecture": Skulls.

p. 27, sidebar: "an electrochemical . . . wine vinegar": Raboy, p. 42.

p. 28: "only fundamental . . . lecture hall": ibid.

p. 28: "electric conflict" and "dispersed pretty widely" and "performs circles": ibid. Also, Forbes, p. 51.

p. 29: "translated into . . . scientific journals": Segre, p. 127.

p. 29: "From the . . . thought about it": ibid.

p. 29: "soon repeated . . . of science": Stauffer, p. 50.

CHAPTER 4: WESTWARD HO!

p. 31: The *West Lashaway* . . . Congolese gold: Bell and Lockerbie (1984), p. 19. Also, Helgason.

p. 31: Stashed in . . . one officer: Bell and Lockerbie (1984), p. 268.

p. 32: Ten thousand . . . World War II: Buff, p. 532.

p. 33: "small but comfortable": Bell and Lockerbie (1984), p. 21.

p. 33: "When we . . . South Atlantic," and "and the joy . . . loved ones.": Bell, E., p. 18.

p. 33: In 1942 . . . British and Americans: Bercuson, p. 15. The United States got the right to operate in the British colony of Trinidad after President Roosevelt loaned the British fifty old destroyers in September 1940. This agreement was called (no surprise) the "Destroyers-for-Bases Deal." The United States was also granted rent-free land in Newfoundland, Bermuda, and on several British-controlled islands in the Caribbean. Construction on the new American base in Trinidad began in January 1941.

Over 10,000 Trinidadian workers helped build the harbors, airfields, and barracks while two hundred Americans worked on malaria reduction (Bercuson, p. 15; Wikipedia, "Naval Base Trinidad").

p. 34: "in his . . . dining room": Bell and Lockerbie (1984), p. 21.

p. 34: "there was no . . . not welcome": ibid., p. 19.

p. 34: "They that go . . . the deep": Bell, E., p. 22.

p. 34: "We knew . . . hunting grounds": ibid., p. 19.

p. 35: Nearly every day . . . bandaged survivors: *New York Times*, "Third Ship," "U-Boats Off Coast," "U-Boat Torpedoes"; Hurd.

p. 35: "the most dangerous . . . entire world": Offley, p. 159.

p. 35, sidebar: France wasn't . . . to Canada: Wikipedia, "Flight"; *Chicago Tribune*.

pp. 35–36: "must be assigned . . . at sea," and "like a sentry . . . at his post": Gannon, p. 415.

p. 36: "The Navy's failure . . . at this stage": Farago, p. 98. Even Samuel Eliot Morison, who was hired by the navy to write its official history of the war, was unwilling to mince words. "This writer cannot avoid the conclusion," he wrote, "that the United States Navy was woefully unprepared, materially and mentally, for the U-boat blitz on the Atlantic Coast that began in January, 1942," and that "this unpreparedness was largely the Navy's own fault" (Morison, p. 200).

p. 37: lacked the tools: Buell, p. 269. In March 1942, Commander Ernest J. King wrote to a fellow officer, "The submarine situation on the east coast approaches the 'desperate.' All in all, we have to do the best we can with what we've got." To another officer, King wrote, "The facts of the matter are that we have not yet got the 'tools' that are necessary to protect shipping in the Eastern Sea Frontier (Florida to Maine)—or anywhere else. Production is months upon months behind schedule" (Buell, p. 269).

p. 37: "tragically . . . and brine": Gannon, p. 338.

p. 37: "inundated . . . all quarters": Buell, p. 269.

p. 37: "not the slipshod . . . well depend": Bell, E., p. 20

p. 37: "to prepare . . . own quarters": Bell and Lockerbie (1984), p. 21.

p. 37: "we had . . . was ours": Whitbeck, "Rainbow," p. 2.

p. 37: "This was so much fun . . . New York City": ibid.

p. 39: "It's impossible . . . to science": Whistler.

p. 38, sidebar: "experienced skippers . . . crews": Morison, p. 268.

p. 38, sidebar: "The Hooligan Navy": ibid., p. 274.

p. 38, sidebar: "Get the . . . scram": Wylie.

CHAPTER 5: MAKING THE CONNECTION

p. 41: "cramped quarters over a stable": Hirshfeld, p. 3.

p. 41: The schoolmistress . . . out of school: Hamilton, pp. 1–2.

p. 41: "strike 1000 blows . . . practice": James, F., *Tales*, p. 236.

p. 42: "delighted in . . . treatises": Thompson, p. 6.

p. 42: "simple experiments": ibid.

p. 42: "copper and zinc . . . storing electricity": Hirshfeld, p. 2.

p. 42: "as many coals . . . he wanted": Arianrhod, p. 119.

p. 42: "permission to . . . own experiments": Hirshfeld, p. 38.

p. 42: "No one . . . to require": James, F., *Tales*, p. 237.

p. 42: "My fear . . . my knowledge," and "increased my boldness": Thompson, p. 76.

p. 43: "like a tiny satellite": Hirshfeld, p. 79.

p. 44: "We have succeeded!": ibid., p. 80.

p. 44: "common place employment": James, F., *Correspondence*, Vol. 1, p. 392.

p. 45: "showman, shaman, and storyteller": Hirshfeld, p. 99.

p. 45: "Always remember . . . the reason": ibid., pp. 101–02.

p. 45: "You know . . . and philosophise": Faraday, *Chemical History*, p. 77. The reason ice floats on water is that when water freezes, it expands and becomes less dense than the water that produced it. That means the water is heavier, and it displaces the lighter ice, causing the ice to float. A pebble on the other hand, will sink, because it is denser than water (ibid., p. 77).

p. 45, sidebar: One day . . . of his lab: Wickman.

p. 45, sidebar: "when the introduction . . . them going": Sacks, p. 166.

p. 46: "expensive . . . to maintain": Hirshfeld, p. 113.

p. 47: "delicately balanced . . . magnetized needle": ibid., p. 115.

p. 47: "as though . . . immediately subsided": ibid., p. 116.

p. 48: "tied together . . . V-shaped 'jaw'": ibid., p. 119.

p. 48: "a mere . . . push or pull": Martin, p. 372.

p. 48: "distinct conversion . . . into Electricity": ibid.

p. 48: "field": Jones, p. 162.

p. 48: "invisible strings": Arianrhod, p. 111.

p. 48: "lines of force": Jones, p. 5.

p. 48: "upon the surface of disturbed water": Moss, p. 394. This quote comes from a letter that has quite a backstory. On March 12, 1832, an unknown person put the letter in a strongbox in London's Royal Society, a sister organization to Faraday's Royal Institution. The Royal Society was founded in 1663 with the goal of "improving Natural Knowledge." Today it is the United Kingdom's national science academy with members including 1,600 of the world's most eminent scientists. Faraday's letter sat at this institution for over one hundred years! The box was finally opened on June 24, 1937. In the letter, Faraday wrote, "I am inclined to compare the diffusion of magnetic forces from a magnetic pole, to the vibrations upon the surface of disturbed water, or those of air in the phenomenon of sound" (The Royal Society).

p. 49: "ray-vibrations": Hirshfeld, p. 167.

p. 50: "tugs . . . of force": ibid., p. 169.

p. 50: "one of . . . scientific mind": Jones, p. 273.

p. 50: "I merely . . . my mind": Faraday, "Thoughts"; Thompson, p. 194.

p. 50: "wandering in a dark labyrinth": Bubo Quote.

p. 50: "God created . . . and measure": Quote Park.

p. 50: "to build . . . the world": Nirenberg, p. 146.

p. 50: "I confess . . . these matters": James, F., *Correspondence*, Vol. 5, p. 219.

p. 50: "It is a . . . too late now": Cross, p. 37.

p. 51: "off the ground . . . cannot walk": Francis.

p. 51: "of appearing . . . world of science": Hirshfeld, p. 171.

p. 51: "by facts placed closely together": James, F., *Correspondence*, Vol. 1, p. 287.

p. 51: "Experiments are . . . fall back upon": Kahlbaum, pp. 199–200.

p. 51, sidebar: "action at a distance": Arianrhod, p. 127.

p. 52: "disobedient to the will": ibid., p. 109.

p. 52: "giddiness and confusion": ibid., p. 314.

p. 52: "so treacherous" and "remember the . . . to the end": ibid., p. 109.

p. 52: "the privilege . . . or thinking": ibid., p. 172.

p. 52: "intensely personal style of working": Forbes, p. 115.

p. 52: "I have seen . . . under these feelings": Thompson, p. 243.

p. 52: "rest content with darkness" and "as dead . . . our thoughts": James, F., *Correspondence*, Vol. 5, p. 245.

p. 52: "How few . . . put forth": Hirshfeld, p. 172.

p. 53: "Where would . . . of the mind?": James, F., *Correspondence*, Vol. 5, p. 246.

p. 53: "left as . . . future ages": James, F., *Correspondence*, Vol. 5, p. 250.

CHAPTER 6: TIN FISH

p. 55: "deadly peril": Hilton, p. 240.

p. 55: "two or possibly three," and "close to Trinidad": Syrett, p. 73.

p. 56: "The day was beautiful" and "the sun . . . of the night": Bell, E., p. 20.

p. 56: "sumptuous noonday dinner": Bell and Lockerbie (1984), p. 21.

p. 56: corned beef and ship's biscuits: Runbeck, p. 177.

p. 56: "memorable slice of pumpkin pie": Bell and Lockerbie (1984), p. 21.

p. 56: "Permission granted": ibid., p. 22.

p. 56: "darted like . . . the sea": Bell, E., p. 21.

p. 56: "were also . . . their cabin": ibid., p. 22.

p. 56: "Torpedo wake . . . amidships" and "Second . . . God": Bell and Lockerbie (1984), p. 23.

p. 56, sidebar: If a captain . . . overboard: Burton.

p. 56, sidebar: In fact . . . U-162: U-Boat Archive, "Report," p. 25.

p. 57: These underwater . . . thirty-five miles per hour: Gannon, p. 3.

p. 57: "tin fish": Bell, E., p. 23.

p. 57: "hit the ship . . . the deck": Whitbeck, "Rainbow," p. 2.

p. 57: "big chunks . . . everywhere": Shaw, p. 121.

p. 57: Carol Shaw . . . "broke [her] right elbow": Stephens, p. 2.

p. 57: "in one act": Bell, E., p. 23.

pp. 57–58: dishes . . . dining room and "We could hardly see": Whitbeck, "Rainbow," p. 2.

p. 58: "Get out! . . . get out": Bell and Lockerbie (1984), p. 52.

p. 58: "As I . . . with the ship": Whitbeck, "Rainbow," p. 3.

p. 58: "sank beneath . . . over my head": Bell, E., p. 24.

p. 58: "I freely . . . was taking in": Whitbeck, "Rainbow," p. 3.

p. 59: "I was sure . . . had come": Bell, E., p. 26.

p. 59: "I shall . . . in heaven": ibid., p. 24.

p. 59: "soon see . . . and Jesus": Whitbeck, "Rainbow," p. 3.

p. 59: "coughing and gagging": Bell and Lockerbie (1984), p. 53.

p. 59: "other forms . . . to identify": ibid.

p. 59: "We hugged . . . each other": Whitbeck, "Rainbow," p. 3.

p. 59: "Mother!": Bell and Lockerbie (1984), p. 53.

p. 59: "Children, over . . . Lord!": ibid.

p. 59: "We swam . . . around us": Bell, E., p. 25.

p. 60: "Over here! . . . here!": Bell and Lockerbie (1984), p. 54.

p. 60: "Help me . . . is wounded," and "Gentle hands . . . lay there": Bell, E., p. 29.

p. 60: He had not . . . another man and "came up . . . save her": Whitbeck, "Rainbow," p. 3.

p. 61: "I thought . . . us all": Bell, E., p. 28.

p. 61: "Anyone seen . . . Bosun": Bell and Lockerbie (1984), p. 59.

p. 61: "Captain's hurt . . . bunch up": ibid.

p. 61: "like a . . . barges": ibid., p. 60.

pp. 61–62: "Best to . . . big brother": ibid., p. 93.

p. 62: "First, men well done . . . we're also taking on water": ibid., p. 60.

pp. 62–63: "All right . . . Mrs. Shaw?" and "Mrs. Shaw . . . Captain" and "burst into sobs" and "I'm sorry . . . over here" and "Aren't you . . . with me": ibid., p. 60.

p. 63: "may have . . . we realized": Bell, E., p. 38.

p. 63: "I'll be . . . to you": Bell and Lockerbie (1984), p. 61.

p. 63: "but the . . . permit it": Bell, E., p. 38.

p. 63: "Go ahead, son": Bell and Lockerbie (1984), p. 61.

p. 63: Seeing Carol's . . . a sling: ibid., p. 66.

p. 63: "What do you think . . . here with me": ibid., p. 61.

p. 63: "Okay, then . . . our supplies": ibid.

p. 64: "Look, there's . . . Grab it": ibid., p. 62.

p. 65: "No way . . . keeping them": ibid., p. 64.

p. 65: "Oh Mother . . . so sick": ibid., p. 67.

p. 65: "Most everyone . . . the side": Whitbeck, "Rainbow," p. 4.

p. 65, sidebar: The word . . . is today: Wikipedia, "Pemmican."

p. 65, sidebar: To stay alive . . . a day: Coleman.

p. 66: "For heaven's sake . . . help it": Bell and Lockerbie (1984), p. 67.

p. 66: "I'm going . . . some company": ibid.

p. 66: "I don't . . . till morning": ibid., pp. 77–78.

p. 66: "Mrs. Bell . . . each other" and "Sure it's . . . if you can": ibid., p. 86.

p. 67: "better reason . . . our prayers": ibid., p. 87.

p. 67: "The Lord . . . not want" and "He maketh . . . soul": ibid., p. 87.

p. 67: "Get comfortable . . . a night": ibid., p. 78.

p. 67: "There was little . . . taken place": Bell, E., pp. 35–37.

p. 67: "One by one . . . at sea'": ibid., p. 37.

p. 67: "If I take . . . shall hold me": ibid.

p. 67: "the longest . . . experienced": ibid.

p. 67: "searched the . . . saw none": ibid., p. 38.

CHAPTER 7: MAXWELL'S EQUATIONS AND HERTZ'S WAVE

p. 69: "He has great work . . . go of it?": Campbell, pp. 15–16.

p. 69: "electromagnetic machines" and "the wonder . . . in space": Forbes, p. 134.

p. 70: "A knowledge . . . the other": ibid., p. 146.

p. 70: "one of . . . of science": ibid., p. 165.

p. 70: "I was at first . . . it so well": James, F., *Correspondence*, Vol. 5, p. 207.

p. 70: "cloaked in . . . symbolism": Hirshfeld, p. 184.

p. 70, sidebar: So he . . . his dormitory: Hirshfeld, p. 179.

p. 71: "gives me much encouragement" and "most probably" and "I wonder . . . with them": James, F., *Correspondence*, Vol. 5, p. 207.

p. 71: The number . . . per second: Campbell, p. 244.

p. 71: "I think . . . to believe": ibid.

p. 71: "first intercommunication" and "mode and habit of thinking" and "will do me . . . again": James, F., *Correspondence*, Vol. 5, p. 305.

p. 71: "whirring clockwork": Hirshfeld, p. 188.

p. 71: "tugs ropes . . . the belfry": ibid., p. 190.

p. 72: "had lapsed into mysticism": Forbes, pp. 211–12.

p. 72: "predicted *electromagnetic waves*" and "to a . . . different world": ibid., pp. 194, 212. Harvard University psychology professor William James wrote that "Round about the accredited and orderly facts of everyday science there ever floats a sort of dust-cloud of exceptional observations" that prove easy for most people "to ignore" or to consider "unimaginable." James added that "Only the born geniuses let themselves be worried and fascinated by these outstanding exceptions." And when "science is renewed, its new formulas often have more of the voice of the exceptions in them than of what were supposed to be the rules" (James, W.).

p. 72: "one of . . . single individual": Potamian, p. 334.

p. 72: "From a . . . same decade": Feynman, pp. 1–11.

p. 72: "The modern . . . to our senses": Dyson.

p. 73: "no indication . . . a laboratory": Forbes, p. 232.

p. 73: "The spirit . . . and example": ibid., p. 239.

p. 73, sidebar: Maxwell thought . . . objects themselves: Everitt, p. 61.

p. 73, sidebar: "although pairs . . . the other": Harman, p. 31.

p. 74: "When he . . . from them": Stewart.

p. 74: "I still felt ambitious" and "interest in . . . become keener": Bryant, p. 8.

p. 74: "Hard at . . . but electromagnetics": Buchwald, p. 182.

p. 74: "It is impossible . . . than ourselves . . .": Edwards. This quote is taken from "On the Relations Between Light and Electricity," a lecture Hertz delivered to the German Association for the Advancement of Natural Sciences and Medicine in Heidelberg, Germany, in 1889.

p. 75: "the most . . . by art": Faraday, *Experimental*, p. 81.

p. 76: "In classical . . . the gods": Segre, p. 181.

p. 77: "Are you ready?": Voss.

p. 78: "Those who . . . marvelous invention": Day.

p. 79: "17:08—Smoke . . . Steamer sunk": U-Boat Archive, "U-66," p. 37.

CHAPTER 8: THE WAIT BEGINS

p. 81: "do him a good turn sometime" and "Poor . . . all I know": Bell and Lockerbie (1984), p. 116.

p. 82: "It's not exactly . . . it'll do": ibid., p. 63.

p. 82: "I can . . . as that": Bell, E., p. 42.

p. 82: "a precious gift": Bell and Lockerbie (1984), p. 97.

p. 83: "How come . . . your sister": ibid., pp. 95–96.

p. 83: "Our Heavenly . . . Amen": ibid., p. 96.

p. 83: "To this day . . . every bite": ibid.

p. 83: "We've drifted . . . give it a try": Bell and Lockerbie (1984), pp. 100–01.

p. 84: "It took . . . headway whatever": ibid., p. 101.

p. 84: "We were wasting . . . later on" and "Nobody . . . decision": ibid.

p. 84: "How about . . . buy that": ibid., p. 104.

p. 84: "Most of . . . stunned him" and "some action . . . be taken": Bell, E., p. 38.

p. 85: "Good work . . . that sail": Bell and Lockerbie (1984), pp. 104–05.

p. 85: "Captain Bogdan . . . canvas" and "When the canvas . . . thoughtful of you": ibid., p. 105.

p. 85: "Throughout the . . . and importance": Bell, E., pp. 41–42.

p. 85: "We'll lash . . . time": Bell and Lockerbie (1984), p. 102.

p. 86: "Why don't . . . more comfortable": ibid.

p. 86: "Maybe it'll hold . . . you hear me?": ibid., pp. 102–03.

p. 86: "Already the . . . not infrequent" and "the closest of friends": Bell, E., pp. 60–61.

p. 87: "Listen up . . . ever see": Bell and Lockerbie (1984), pp. 118–19.

p. 87: "Everyone was . . . wondering": Bell, E., p. 37.

p. 87: "When do . . . stinkin' raft" and "Oh God . . . wanna die!": Bell and Lockerbie (1984), pp. 109–10.

p. 87, sidebar: "Glacier Cream": Mertes; *New York Times*, "Sunscreen."

p. 88: "He thought . . . Psalm 23": Whitbeck, "Rainbow," p. 6.

p. 88: "just sat" and "looked wistful and lonely": Bell, E., p. 62.

p. 88: "What do . . . the rations?": Bell and Lockerbie (1984), p. 121.

p. 88: "Remember, men . . . as before": ibid.

pp. 88–89: "You know what . . . made of?" and "Bake . . . Yessiree!": ibid., pp. 125–42. Note: The dialogue in this section is a composite from two rounds of the food game reported by Bell and Lockerbie.

p. 89: "Damned stupid": ibid., p. 130.

p. 89: "a way . . . rations were" and "From that . . . took strength": ibid., pp. 130–31.

p. 90: "It hurts too much to pray!": ibid., p. 135.

p. 90: "Don't let . . . like that" and "Aye, aye, captain": ibid.

p. 90: "No way . . . my order": ibid., p. 131.

p. 90: "Nobody . . . the men be": ibid.

p. 90: What Peifer didn't . . . to its target: Conger.

p. 90, sidebar: Salmon and . . . spawning grounds: Briggs; Baltazar-Soares.

CHAPTER 9: HUMBLE BEGINNING

p. 93: "so an . . . is reflected": Fisher, D., p. 69.

p. 93: "to determine . . . at sea": Cheney, p. 259.

p. 93: "The scientific . . . taken up": Tesla, p. 119.

p. 93: "The first . . . another rejection: Fisher, D., pp. 42–43.

p. 94: Twelve years later . . . *Nein*: ibid., p. 43.

p. 94: "If [a ship] . . . been solved": Secor, p. 270.

p. 94: "would certainly . . . dream stuff": Cheney, p. 260.

pp. 94–95: "It seems . . . direction" and "and thereby . . . or thick weather": Allison, p. 54.

p. 95: "an astounding announcement": Raboy, p. 473.

p. 95: Leo Young . . . Illinois: Allison, pp. 43–45.

p. 95, sidebar: In 1909 . . . Oscilloscope: Raboy, p. 305.

p. 95, sidebar: The Ohio-born . . . purposes: Kantha, p. 436.

p. 96: Dr. Taylor . . . ingenuity: ibid., pp. 41–45.

p. 96: "the brains and the ideas" and "to follow through with them": ibid., p. 45.

p. 96: "a little shack . . . in Washington, DC": Page, R., p. 19.

p. 96: "We noticed . . . approximate location": Taylor, p. 91.

p. 97: "realized that . . . extremely useful": Allison, p. 39.

p. 97: "filter" and "without detection": Taylor, p. 91.

p. 97: "the detection . . . by radio": ibid.

p. 97: In 1933 . . . million radios: Encyclopedia.com, "Radio 1929–1941."

p. 98: "bombing aeroplanes . . . civilization" and "is inexcusable": Clark, *Tizard*, p. 107. British leaders wondered, *How do we counter such a threat?* Stanley Baldwin, a former prime minister, was not optimistic. In a speech to the House of Commons in November 1932, he said, "I think it is well for the man in the street to realize that there is no power on earth that can protect him from being bombed. Whatever people may tell him, the bomber will always get through." Baldwin's pessimism stemmed from Britain's experience in World War I when its "early warning system" consisted of 200-foot-long concrete "sound mirrors" carved into sea cliffs and a band of "blind people with acute senses of hearing" listening through ear trumpets for the sound of incoming planes (Buderi, p. 52).

p. 98: "More work . . . receivers" and "far enough . . . investigation": Allison, pp. 62–63.

p. 98: "matter of the utmost importance": ibid., p. 63.

p. 99: Over the next year . . . consequences: Allison, 64; Guerlac, p. 69.

p. 99: "obvious weaknesses" and "outright antagonism": Guerlac, p. 70.

p. 99: "we'll cancel it out": Allison, p. 92.

p. 99: "The decision . . . the project": ibid., p. 79.

p. 100: "be of useful . . . fellow man": ibid., p. 86.

p. 100: "complete flop": ibid., p. 87.

p. 100: "extraordinary . . . of invention": Taylor, 173. Taylor goes on to say that Robert Page contributed "more new ideas to the field of radar than any other one man."

p. 100: "had more . . . had fleas": Allison, p. 87.

p. 100: "This is . . . figure it out": ibid., p. 82.

p. 101: The scope . . . "pips": Fisher, D., p. 114; Bellis.

p. 101: "its first . . . December 1934": Allison, p. 2.

p. 101: "blind alley": Guerlac, p. 73.

p. 101: "was promising enough to go on": Allison, p. 2. Radar historian Robert Buderi wrote that the Page–Young test in December 1934 "proved the feasibility of a pulsed system a full month before. . . [British physicist] Watson-Watt even dreamed of radar" (ibid., p. 63).

p. 101: "extremely low priority": Guerlac, p. 73.

p. 101: "series of . . . so on": Allison, p. 93.

p. 101: "communication": ibid., p. 90. Taylor wrote, "This radar work had been supported by very pitiful funds diverted perhaps illegally, I will admit, from other projects. The time had arrived when we definitely needed more tangible support." In early 1935, Taylor went to Capitol Hill to talk to Nevada Congressman James Scrugham, who was both a student of engineering and the most influential member of the Naval Appropriations Subcommittee. Afterward the congressman asked a few questions but promised nothing. Taylor said he left the Capitol feeling "very much discouraged," but the following week, Scrugham called to tell Taylor the subcommittee had agreed to give $100,000 to the radar project. Taylor wrote that "it looked like ten million dollars to us then" (ibid., p. 90).

pp. 101–102: "Success came immediately" and "The echoes . . . transmitted": Allison, p. 94.

p. 102: "I was . . . elated" and "I realized . . . defence": Kinsey, p. 138.

p. 102: "demonstrated . . . be detected": Watson-Watt, *Pulse*, p. 65.

p. 103: Page . . . 250 feet: Page, R., p. 80.

p. 103: "highest possible priority" and "a confidential . . . category": Guerlac, p. 77. According to naval historian Vincent Davis, Rear Admiral Harold Bowen was an "innovation advocate." Such people, Davis explained, "have frequently been responsible for winning adoption of new technical programs, often in the face of entrenched opposition. Although seldom inventors themselves, they usually have the technical background to understand advances better than their colleagues." This was true of Bowen, who had earned a master's degree in mechanical engineering from Columbia University in 1914 (Allison, pp. 132–33).

p. 103: "at the earliest possible date": Brown, L., p. 66.

p. 103: "utterly impossible . . . no way": Allison, p. 100.

p. 104: "receiver would . . . transmitter": Page, R., p. 122.

p. 104: "Well, think . . . be a way." Allison, p. 100.

p. 104: "he apparently . . . the minister": Page, J.

p. 104: "I only . . . guided by it": Page, R., pp. 124–25.

p. 104: "It worked . . . was tried": ibid., p. 122.

pp. 104–105: "Like so . . . radar" and "Page's . . . duplexer" and "exercise his talent": Allison, p. 100.

p. 105: The problem . . . too weak: ibid., p. 102.

p. 105: "completed on . . . Feb. 1938": ibid., p. 103.

p. 105: "equaled our dreams": Page, R., p. 133.

p. 106: Young positioned . . . speculation: Guerlac, p. 84; Allison, p. 105.

p. 106: "flying bedspring": Allison, p. 105.

p. 106: "spectacular": Page, R., p. 133.

p. 106: "standing guard against surprise" and "far . . . tactics" and "be installed . . . vessels" and "The device. . . it occupies": Guerlac, pp. 87–88.

p. 106: Second, with . . . over Britain: Royal Air Force Museum. The Royal Air Force that defeated Hitler's *Luftwaffe* in the Battle of Britain was a diverse bunch. In addition to the roughly 2,300 British pilots, there were 145 Poles, 126 New Zealanders, 98 Canadians, 88 Czechoslovakians, 33 Australians, 29 Belgians, 25 South Africans, 13 French, 3 Rhodesians, and one each from Austria, Jamaica, Barbados, and Newfoundland (ibid.).

p. 106, sidebar: "Navy Needs . . . confidential equipment": *Richmond Times Dispatch*.

p. 107: "We were . . . twelve miles": Bell and Lockerbie (1984), p. 50.

p. 107: "delayed, perhaps missing": ibid., p. 181.

p: 107: "Well, that . . . go searching": ibid., p. 182.

CHAPTER 10: GOING SOLO

p. 109: "I agree, captain . . . aye, sir" and "Listen up . . . Mr. Greenwell" and "There was no . . . separating might mean.": Bell and Lockerbie (1984), pp. 166–67.

p. 110: "Good luck . . . New York": ibid., p. 167.

p. 110: "to take good care of Carol": ibid., p. 67.

p. 110: "We'd go up . . . rafts disappear": ibid., p. 167.

p. 110: "I was numb . . . so fast": ibid., pp. 167–168.

p. 110: "that nothing happened": ibid., p. 175.

p. 110: "Remember . . . ice box out there": ibid., p. 176.

p. 110: "I fell . . . of our situation": ibid.

p. 110: "One time . . . in the dark": ibid.

p. 111: "going a-fishing": Bell, E., p. 69.

p. 111: "The children . . . watching him": ibid.

p. 111: You are . . . only sunshine: Bell and Lockerbie (1984), p. 199.

p. 111, sidebar: "a sewer pipe with valves": Gannon, p. 5.

p. 111, sidebar: Various valves . . . clean up: ibid., pp. 423–24.

p. 112: "Just as . . . our tonic": ibid.

p. 112: "I think . . . was torpedoed": Bell, E., p. 62.

p. 112: "His end . . . solemn thing": ibid., p. 63.

p. 112: "What could . . . the deceased": ibid., p. 64.

p. 112: "Men, I'm . . . of us": Bell and Lockerbie (1984), p. 194.

p. 112: "face the . . . might hold": Bell, E., p. 64.

p. 112: "prayed briefly": ibid.

p. 112: "Heavenly Father": Bell and Lockerbie (1984), p. 194.

p. 112, sidebar 2: "singing it . . . named 'Sunshine'": Deusner.

p. 113: "They musn't get . . . to the bottom": ibid., pp. 200–202.

p. 114: "For a moment . . . had gone": Bell, E., p. 66.

p. 114: "He was . . . ever knew": Bell and Lockerbie (1984), p. 204.

p. 114: "yet never . . . behalf of us all": ibid., p. 103.

p. 114: "watch over us" and "bring us to safety soon": ibid., p. 204.

p. 114: "serious blow . . . morale" and "meant something" and "the men . . . happen": ibid., p. 203.

p. 114: "Listen up . . . from me": ibid., p. 205.

p. 114: "Says who, Peifer?" and "I'm the . . . on board": ibid.

p. 115: "Yea, but . . . knows it": ibid.

p. 115: "Okay, Mrs. Bell . . . heard me, Mrs. Bell": ibid., pp. 204–05.

p. 115: "He was . . . harm us": Whitbeck, "Rainbow, Part Two," p. 2.

p. 115: "Mr. Peifer, I refuse to move" and "Don't never . . . without rations": Bell and Lockerbie (1984), p. 206.

p. 115: "God's message . . . something beautiful": ibid., p. 207.

p. 115: "God—God . . . all be dead!": ibid., p. 173.

p. 116: "You mark . . . your space": ibid., p. 206.

p. 116: "*Unto the . . . whence arise?*": ibid., p. 174.

p. 116: "I was scared . . . saved us": ibid., p. 255.

p. 116: "But even . . . salt water": Bell, E., p. 46.

p. 116: "Listen, everybody . . . sundown tomorrow": Bell and Lockerbie (1984), p. 224.

p. 116: "I don't remember . . . directly overhead": ibid., p. 225.

p. 117: "We could see . . . the windows": Bell, E., p. 87.

p. 117: "We . . . probably   been room": ibid., p. 86.

p. 117: "Easy does it! . . . in the water": Bell and Lockerbie (1984), p. 225.

p. 117: "struck the . . . a brick": Bell, E., p. 226.

p. 117: "Down it . . . straight dive": ibid., p. 87.

p. 117: "we could see the airmen's faces": Whitbeck, "Rainbow, Part Two," p. 2.

p. 117: "probably their . . . rations": ibid.

p. 117: "The airmen . . . next day": ibid.

p. 117: "That night . . . my memory": Bell, E., p. 88.

p. 118: "Do you think . . . the first place": Bell and Lockerbie (1984), p. 227.

p. 118: "a chair . . . to sleep?": Bell, E., p. 89.

p. 118: "We had our prayers and breakfast": ibid., p. 90.

p. 118: "obviously searching": Whitbeck, "Rainbow, Part Two," p. 3.

p. 118: "two or three . . . from deliverance": Bell and Lockerbie (1984), p. 229.

p. 118: "We watched . . . and fears": Bell, E., p. 90.

p. 118: "Hey, what's . . . your eyes": Bell and Lockerbie (1984), p. 229.

p. 119: "We could tell . . . have been": ibid., p. 230.

p. 119: "a sickening of the heart" and "only a smudge of smoke": Bell, E., pp. 90–91.

p. 119: "our hopes and spirits": Whitbeck, "Rainbow, Part Two," p. 3.

p. 119: "very primitive, still experimental": Bell and Lockerbie (1984), p. 50.

CHAPTER 11: MICROWAVES

p. 121: At two-forty . . . his copilot: U-Boat Archive, "*Topa Topa*." The *Topa Topa* was hit at 2:37 in the morning, but it didn't sink until 4:02. In Trinidad, Donald Gay heard about the sinking on the day it happened, so it's reasonable to assume that the radio operator on the *Topa Topa* sent a distress call a few minutes after the torpedoes hit. When the *Sir Huon* was hit the next day, the radio operator sent a distress call in the twenty-five minutes between impact and sinking. We know this because many years later, the radio man on U-66 told Robert Bell that he had heard that call (Bell and Lockerbie (1984), p. 49; U-Boat Archive, "Topa Topa"; U-Boat Archive, "Sir Huon").

p. 122: "our wings overlapped": Bell and Lockerbie (1984), p. 50.

p. 123: "If automobiles . . . of gas": Alvarez, p. 83.

p. 123: "the most . . . our shores": Wilkins, p. 505.

p. 123: One of the inventors . . . experiment: Lazarus, p. 115.

p. 123: "with some . . . radar activities" and "stuck in my mind": ibid., p. 115.

p. 123: Back at the university . . . form of radio waves: Buderi, p. 84.

p. 124, sidebar: "Out! . . . reserved": Bowen, p. 154.

p. 125, sidebar: "submachine guns . . . orifice": ibid., p. 155.

p. 125: "clothed in . . . discharge," and "became uncomfortably warm," and "in an attempt . . . produced": Cockburn, p. 85.

p. 125: "hoping they . . . illumination": Blair, *Hunters*, p. 129.

p. 125: "lamps of . . . power": Cockburn, p. 85.

p. 125: "We were astonished": Lazarus, p. 115.

p. 125: "it was an easy . . . hundred-fold!" Blair, *Hunters*, p. 129.

p. 126: "It is impossible . . . Boot's work" and "electronic stone age": ibid.

p. 126: "That day . . . in the war": Clark, *Boffins*, p. 131. British physicist M. H. F. Wilkins echoed those thoughts when he wrote in 1987 that "the cavity magnetron . . . was probably the most decisive contribution of science to the winning of World War II" (Wilkins, p. 493).

p. 126: Three months later . . . seven miles away: Blair, *Hunters*, p. 129. Professor David Fisher explains that "the basic concept of the magnetron is to use a magnetic field to herd the electrons along, to guide them where you want them to go. Randall and Boot combined this with a totally different concept—the concept of a penny whistle." Such a whistle consists of a loose hard ball in a cavity. The force of the blowing makes the little ball vibrate, and those vibrations generate sound waves, which reverberate inside the cavity and then escape. The size of the cavity and the frequency with which the sound waves reverberate determine the type of sound emitted from the whistle. Fisher notes that a big whistle emits a "low-pitched hoot" while a tiny whistle emits a "high-pitched scream." The cavity magnetron is like a tiny whistle. But instead of sound waves reverberating inside a cavity, it's electrons. As the electrons bounce back and forth in the cavities, they emit electromagnetic waves. The precise measurements of the cavities mean the electrons move only a few centimeters between bounces, and therefore produce "high-pitched" microwaves (Fisher, D., pp. 249–50).

p. 126: "the first . . . radar history": Buderi, p. 105.

p. 127: On August . . . further orders: De Chair, p. 133. Captain de Chair received another order forbidding him to buy eggs on the black market. All eggs, he was told, had to be bought from official military vendors, all of whom insisted on 48 hours advance notice. De Chair wrote, "After nine months in the Freetown Escort Force, which seldom necessitated spending more than 24 hours in harbour for fuel, we consequently never got any eggs, and the desire for them became an obsession" (De Chair, p. 133).

p. 127, sidebar: Edward Bowen . . . New Mexico: Buderi, p. 47.

p. 127, sidebar: "the physicists' war": Kaiser, p. 523.

CHAPTER 12: ANSWERED PRAYERS

p. 129: "less than . . . left": Whitbeck, "Rainbow, Part Two," p. 3. On day sixteen, by looking at the water keg, Mary could see that there was less than two gallons left (256 ounces). If each of the seventeen people drank two ounces per day, that would add up to sixty-eight ounces after two days. So by the end of day seventeen, there would've been less than 188 ounces left.

p. 129: The bosun said . . . "wee drop more": Bell, E., p. 93.

p. 129: "a dangerous practice" and "since one's last . . . were obtained": ibid., p. 94.

p. 129: "Food had . . . my mouth": ibid., p. 93.

pp. 129–130: "ask God . . . us rain" and "at the . . . request" and "a convenience . . . and served": ibid., p. 94.

p. 130: "asked our . . . our direction": ibid., p. 95.

p. 130: "the windows . . . were opened": ibid., p. 95.

p. 131: "I had seen . . . like this": Bell and Lockerbie (1984), p. 232.

p. 131: "It pelted . . . refreshment": Bell, E., p. 96.

p. 131: "Every few . . . without cessation": ibid.

p. 131: "we basked . . . and praise": ibid., pp. 96–97.

p. 132: "with relish": ibid., 70.

p. 132: "I do not remember . . . liking it": Stephens, p. 2.

p. 132: "does remember . . . liking it": Bell and Lockerbie (1996), p. 188. After being adopted, Carol Shaw changed her name to Donna Hobson. After getting married, she became Donna Hobson Taylor (Stephens, pp. 3–4).

p. 132: "caught no more fish": Bell, E., p. 70.

p. 132: "angry hue": ibid., p. 75.

p. 132: "floated temporarily": Whitbeck, "Rainbow, Part Two," p. 4.

p. 132: Incredibly . . . intact: Bell, E., p. 77; Whitbeck, "Rainbow, Part Two," p. 4.

p. 132, sidebar: Sharks and pilot fish . . . relationship: Wikipedia, "Pilot Fish."

p. 133: Flavor claimed . . . calm him: Bell and Lockerbie (1984), p. 240.

p. 133: "that some . . . breaking point": Bell, E., p. 101.

p. 133: "animal impulses": Bell and Lockerbie (1984), p. 239.

p. 133: "We're done . . . Look at us": ibid., p. 240.

CHAPTER 13: DESTINATION TRINIDAD

p. 135: Twenty-five days . . . new orders: U-Boat Archive "HMS Vimy."

p. 135: "proceeded to . . . submarine attacks": De Chair, p. 143.

p. 135: "Having handed . . . following morning": ibid., p. 145.

p. 136: "maneuvered wildly . . . just barely": Blair, *Hunters*, p. 683.

p. 136: "the hunt was on": De Chair, p. 145.

p. 136: The senior British . . . sailed eastward: Blair, *Hunters*, p. 684.

p. 136: "pitch dark": De Chair, p. 145.

p. 136: "large surface vessel": ibid.

p. 136: "opened fire from 'A' gun": ibid.

p. 136: "full speed": ibid.

p. 136: "which did not deceive us": ibid., p. 146.

p. 137: Hearing a . . . its owner: ibid.

p. 137: One German . . . the dark: U-Boat Archive "Action," p. 3.

p. 137: "some kind of location device": Padfield, p. 242.

p. 137: These interrogations . . . no traitors · ibid., p. 274. Padfield wrote that Dönitz's investigation "turned up indiscreet French liaisons but no traitor."

p. 137: Captain de Chair . . . laundry: Fairweather, p. 178. While in Trinidad, de Chair received a telegram from none other than the Commander in Chief of the United States Fleet, Ernest King. It said: "MY CONGRATULATIONS ON THE FINE WORK OF *VIMY* IN ABOLISHING ANOTHER GERMAN SUBMARINE." (National Archives, "Post Mortems").

p. 137: "so dear to the heart": Fairweather, p. 178.

p. 138: Four days later . . . Boca di Navios: Bell and Lockerbie (1984), p. 235.

p. 138: sidebar: "An irascible . . . 'git'": Moore, p. 65.

p. 138: sidebar: "I thought . . . Yankees!": ibid.

p. 139: "Chief, some of us . . . That's all there is! That's all": ibid., pp. 241–243.

p. 139: "The prospect . . . too bright": Bell, E., pp. 103–104.

p. 139: "Only then . . . we were": Bell and Lockerbie (1984), p. 243.

p. 140: The *Vimy* had just . . . found the raft: ibid., p. 244.

p. 140: "innovation advocates": Allison, p. 132.

p. 140: "Object bearing . . . five miles" and "U-boat on the surface": Bell and Lockerbie (1984), p. 244.

p. 140: "I grabbed . . . the slightest doubt": ibid.

pp. 140–141: "Convoy!" and "They're coming . . . see for yourself": ibid.

p. 141: "Never till . . . missing us": Bell, E., p. 104.

p. 141: "Attack at all possible speed": Bell and Lockerbie (1984), p. 244.

p. 141: "When we saw . . . streamlined bow": Bell, E., p. 104.

p. 142: "Fire A-gun! . . . gun!": Bell and Lockerbie (1984), p. 245.

p. 142: "It was . . . of despair": Whitbeck, "Rainbow, Part Two," p. 4.

p. 142: "All our hard . . . over our heads": Bell, E., p. 105.

p. 142: "Oh God . . . this way!": Bell and Lockerbie (1984), p. 245.

p. 142: "screamed in terror," and "down in . . . the raft": Bell, E., p. 105.

p. 142: "upper works" and "a dirty white flag": De Chair, p. 148.

p. 142: "the object . . . conning tower" and "People packed . . . shot away" and "As we drew . . . pathetic sight": ibid., pp. 148–49.

p. 142: "Who are you?" and "We're Americans!": Bell and Lockerbie (1984), p. 246.

p. 142: "We're survivors . . . torpedoed ship": Bell, E., p. 106.

p. 143: "You sons . . . right now": Bell and Lockerbie (1984), p. 246.

p. 143: "wonderful sight" and "I still get goose bumps": Whitbeck, "Rainbow, Part Two," p. 5.

p. 143: "ran for . . . sprayed bullets": Bell and Lockerbie (1984), p. 246.

p. 143: "just being themselves": Venables.

p. 143: "He seemed surprisingly fit": Bell and Lockerbie (1984), p. 246.

p. 143: "Hands reached . . . past unbelievable": Whitbeck, "Rainbow, Part Two," p. 5.

p. 143: "I'm glad you picked us up": Stephens, p. 4.

p. 143: The two . . . years later: ibid.; Bell and Lockerbie (1984), pp. 264–65.

p. 143: "big, comfortable . . . my back": Bell, E., p. 106.

p. 143: "that those Brits . . . rum": Bell and Lockerbie (1984), p. 261.

p. 143: Doctors arrived . . . in Trinidad: ibid., p. 248.

p. 144: "The British . . . to us" and "the last . . . the *Vimy*": ibid., p. 248.

p. 145: Even with . . . the ropes: ibid., pp. 248–249. Joe Greenwell recalled, "The sea was moderate, with swells two to three feet, but even so, there was enough rise and fall between the *Vimy* and the *Prins Willem* to make our transfer a problem" (ibid.).

p. 145: "Our last view . . . good wishes": Bell, E., pp. 108–09.

p. 145: The steward strawberry jam: Bell and Lockerbie (1984), p. 249.

p. 145: "I remember . . . on the ground": Bell and Lockerbie (1984), p. 250.

pp. 145–146: "We were . . . a raft" and "the longest . . . and children": Whitbeck, "Rainbow, Part Two," p. 6.

p. 146: "the laughter . . . was ended": Bell, E., p. 113.

p. 146: The doctors . . . cut it all off: Bell and Lockerbie (1984), p. 254; Bell, E., p. 32.

p. 146: "I decided . . . my birthday": Whitbeck, "Rainbow, Part Two," pp. 3 & 6.

p. 146: "Her being . . . of us all": Bell and Lockerbie (1984), p. 255.

p. 146: "She saved . . . rain come": Runbeck, p. 182.

p. 146: "God helps . . . help themselves": Bell and Lockerbie (1984), p. 251.

p. 146: "the hero of the story": ibid.

p. 146: "deserves great . . . picked up": ibid.

p. 147: Robert Bell . . . harbor: ibid., p. 254.

p. 147: Richard said . . . gained ten: Shaw, p. 123.

p. 147: Mary Bell . . . different family: Bell and Lockerbie (1984), p. 254.

p. 147: Mrs. Bell . . . knit perfectly": Bell, E., p. 41.

p. 147: "brave little soldier": ibid.

p. 147: The hospital bill . . . Indiana: Bell and Lockerbie (1984), p. 256.

p. 147: "I didn't think . . . but now I do": Shaw, p. 125.

p. 147: Both Shaw children . . . Iowa: Stephens, pp. 3–4.

p. 147: Following a . . . four years: Bell and Lockerbie (1984), p. 256.

p. 148: "official debriefing . . . agencies": ibid., p. 257.

p. 148: When those meetings . . . parents: ibid.

p. 148: On Halloween . . . a costume: ibid.

p. 148: "rushed into . . . U-boat peril": Buderi, p. 153.

p. 148: "the U-boat menace" and "our worst danger": Roskill, p. 138.

p. 148: Roosevelt met . . . planes": ibid.

p. 148: British . . . Liberators: Loewenheim, p. 283, footnote 3.

p. 148: In May . . . 38 U-boats: Buderi, p. 167.

p. 148: "can carry . . . at night": Fuehrer Conferences, p. 331.

p. 149: "losses are too high": ibid., p. 329.

p. 149: "submarine warfare . . . effective": ibid., p. 334.

p. 149: "new detection . . . not familiar": ibid., pp. 335–36.

p. 149: "We don't . . . locates us," ibid., p. 332.

p. 149: "the temporary . . . of our enemies": Lovell, p. 162.

p. 149: That summer . . . was torpedoed: Buderi, p. 168.

p. 149: "although far . . . the war": Encyclopedia.com, "Turning Points."

CHAPTER 14: RECONCILIATION

p. 151: On September . . . survived: Bell and Lockerbie (1984), p. 252.

p. 151: "an envelope . . . Harvey Shaw": ibid., p. 253.

p. 151: "The missionary . . . to pray": Stephens, p. 5.

p. 151: The other two rafts were never found: Bell., E., p. 118. Mrs. Bell wrote "that the other three rafts and their occupants" were never found. She apparently was unaware that a raft from the *West Lashaway* had washed ashore on the island of St. Vincent (ibid.).

p. 151: "Here, readers . . . happened": Runbeck, p. 35.

p. 151: "God had . . . gloriously fulfilled": Bell, E., p. 118.

p. 152: During the first . . . Robert followed: Bell and Lockerbie (1984), pp. 257–58.

p. 152: "gentle little Ethel Bell": Runbeck, p. 35.

p. 152: sailed off again . . . children: Bell and Lockerbie (1984), p. 258.

p. 152: Robert also . . . New York: Legacy.com.

p. 152: except for an . . . to his students: ibid.

p. 153: At a banquet . . . Virginia: Bell and Lockerbie (1984), p. 259.

p. 153: "That was . . . its details": ibid., pp. 259–60.

p. 153: Among the experts . . . addresses: ibid., pp. 260 & 268.

p. 153: "great curiosity . . . my experience" and "no vindictive motive" and "each side . . . is over": ibid., p. 272.

p. 153: "no clear . . . or answered": ibid., p. 271.

p. 153: "I am happy . . . your life": ibid., p. 275.

p. 154: "I am very sorry . . . terrible time": ibid., p. 272.

p. 154: "Often, after . . . were saved": ibid., p. 275.

p. 154: As it turned out . . . did not: Blair, *Hunted*, pp. 547–48.

p. 154: "Mr. Bell . . . to see us" and "Please take . . . a memento" and "I hope . . . good memory": Bell and Lockerbie (1984), p. 283.

p. 154: The following year . . . in 1979): Bell and Lockerbie (1984), pp. 284 & 286.

p. 154: "a man deeply . . . submarine attacks": ibid., p. 277.

p. 154: It's a sad truth . . . decent men": ibid., p. 279.

p. 155: "I am now . . . agree": Kahn, p. 81.

p. 155: "to shake . . . with us" and "a highlight of our lives." ibid., p. 80.

p. 155: "Enemies Become Friends": ibid.

p. 155: sidebar: "The war . . . of the world": Gannon, p. 137.

p. 155: sidebar: "For the first . . . the U.S.A.": Goldstein.

p. 155: sidebar: "I was . . . for Hitler": ibid.

p. 155: sidebar: Hardegen . . . years old: ibid.

CHAPTER 15: EIGHT DECADES OF RADAR

p. 157: The same year the war ended . . . first microwave oven: Hiskey.

p. 158: "pencil beams": Federal Aviation Administration.

p. 158: President Harry . . . by CGA: ibid.

p. 158: sidebar: "How did . . . by radar?" and "You may be . . . radar" and "driving . . . excessive speed": Watson-Watt, *Three Steps*, p. 285.

p. 158: sidebar: "Had I known . . . invented it!": Dingwall.

p. 159: Martin Cooper . . . $3,995: Court.

p. 159: It was Michigan . . . speed limits: Pavlovich.

p. 160: called the device a plipper: Torchinsky.

p. 161: "that warns . . . changing lanes": Halpert. This system was invented by Delco Electronics, which adapted radar technology used on F-15 fighter jets (ibid.).

p. 161: With the new technology . . . of 1942: SeaLevelRise.org.

EPILOGUE

p. 163: Except for . . . age ninety: Bell and Lockerbie (1984), p. 258.

p. 163: "a multitude of great-grandchildren": Roper & Sons.

p. 163: Robert Bell . . . grandchildren: Legacy.com.

p. 164: "looked *into* . . . the earth": Fisher, H., p. 2.

p. 164: "As far . . . Bogdan and me": Bell and Lockerbie (1984), p. 268.

p. 164: In 2016 . . . making the search: Birdsong.

SELECTED BIBLIOGRAPHY

Researching this book took me to libraries, museums, bookstores, and archives in London; Boston; Washington, DC; San Marino, California; and College Park, Maryland. I also received plenty of editorial assistance and scientific guidance from gracious professors at Harvard, Cornell, University of Southern California, and University of Massachusetts at Dartmouth. Below is a selected bibliography created from my full list.

Allison, David K. *New Eye for the Navy: The Origin of Radar at the Naval Research Laboratory*. Washington, DC: Naval Research Laboratory, 1981.

Alvarez, Luis W. *Adventures of a Physicist*. New York: Basic Books, Inc., 1987.

Arianrhod, Robyn. *Einstein's Heroes: Imagining the World through the Language of Mathematics*. New York: Oxford University Press, 2005.

Aryee, Golda. "Korle Lagoon." *Water Bodies* (blog), September 14, 2013. http://waterbodiesgh.blogspot.com/2013/09/korle-lagoon-is-lake-which-is-situated.html.

Baltazar-Soares, Miguel, and Christophe Eizaguirre. "Animal Navigation: The Eel's Magnetic Guide to the Gulf Stream." *Current Biology* 27, no. 12 (June 19, 2017): pp. R604–R606. https://doi.org/10.1016/j.cub.2017.04.042.

Bell, Ethel, as told to J. H. Hunter. *Adrift: The Story of Twenty Days on a Raft in the South Atlantic*. New York: Evangelical Publishers, 1943.

Bell, Robert W., and D. Bruce Lockerbie. *In Peril on the Sea: A Personal Remembrance*. New York: Garden City, 1984.

Bell, Robert W., and D. Bruce Lockerbie. *In Peril on the Sea: The Story of Ethel Bell and Her Children Mary and Robert*, abridged. Camp Hill, PA: Christian Publishing, 1996.

Bellis, Mary. "Karl Ferdinand Braun." Theinventors.org, 2006. https://theinventors.org/library/inventors/blkarlbraun.htm.

Bercuson, David J., and Holger H. Herwig. *Long Night of the Tankers: Hitler's War Against Caribbean Oil*. Calgary, Canada: University of Calgary Press, 2014.

Birdsong, Gene. "SS West Lashaway." TreasureNet.com, October 16, 2016. https://www.treasurenet.com/threads/ss-west-lashaway.518502.

Blair, Clay. *Hitler's U-Boat War: The Hunters, 1939–1942*. New York: Random House, 1996.

———. *Hitler's U-Boat War: The Hunted, 1942–1945*. New York: Random House, 1998.

Bowen, E. G. *Radar Days*. Bristol, England: Adam Hilger, 1987.

Briggs, Helen. "Sockeye Salmon 'Sense Magnetic Field of Home.'" BBC News, February 7, 2013. https://www.bbc.com/news/science-environment-21345259.

Brown, Louis. *A Radar History of World War II: Technical and Military Imperatives*. Philadelphia: Institute of Physics Publishing, 1999.

Bryant, John H. *Heinrich Hertz, The Beginning of Microwaves: Discovery of Electromagnetic Waves and Opening of the Electromagnetic Spectrum by Heinrich Hertz in the Years 1886–1892*. New York: Institute of Electrical and Electronics Engineers, 1998.

Bubo Quote. "Galileo Galilei." https://www.buboquote.com/en/quote/3927-galilei-philosophy-is-written-in-this-grand-book-which-stands-continually-open-before-our-eyes-i.

Buchwald, Jed. *The Creation of Scientific Effects: Heinrich Hertz and Electric Waves.* Chicago: University of Chicago Press, 1994.

Buderi, Robert. *The Invention that Changed the World: How a Small Group of Radar Pioneers Won the Second World War and Launched a Technical Revolution.* New York: Simon & Schuster, 1996.

Buell, Thomas B. *Master of Sea Power: A Biography of Fleet Admiral Ernest J. King.* Boston: Little, Brown and Company, 1980.

Buff, Rachel Ida. "The Deportation Terror." *American Quarterly* 60, no. 3 (September 2008): 523–51.

Burman, Ben Lucien. "The Vichy Men of Africa." *St. Louis Post Dispatch,* March 4, 1942.

Burton, Peter. "A Sailing Trip Aboard the Schooner Mary M. Lewis from Bridgetown to Georgetown–Summer 1939." *Bajan Things* (blog), November 19, 2018. https://www.bajanthings.com/a-sailing-trip-aboard-the-schooner-mary-m-lewis-from-bridgetown-to-georgetown-summer-1939.

Campbell, Lewis, and William Garnett. *The Life of James Clerk Maxwell.* London: Macmillan and Co., 1892.

Cheney, Margaret. *Tesla: Man Out of Time.* New York: Simon and Schuster, 1981.

Chicago Tribune. "Resume Large Gold Shipments from England." July 10, 1940.

Clark, Ronald W. *The Rise of the Boffins.* London: Phoenix House LTD, 1962.

———. *Tizard.* Cambridge, MA: MIT Press, 1965.

Clarke, Arthur C. *Profiles of the Future: An Inquiry into the Limits of the Possible.* London: Victor Gollancz Ltd., 1962.

Cockburn, Stewart, and David Ellyard. *Oliphant: The Life and Times of Sir Mark Oliphant.* Adelaide, Australia: Axiom Books, 1981.

Coleman, Erin. "Calorie Requirements for Men & Women." SFGATE.com. https://healthyeating.sfgate.com/calorie-requirements-men-women-9428.html.

Comhaire, Jean L., Nancy Ellen Lawler, and Robert John Mundt. "Côte d'Ivoire." *Encyclopedia Britannica,* November 5, 2022. https://www.britannica.com/place/Cote-dIvoire.

Conger, Cristen. "What Is Electroreception and How Do Sharks Use It?" HowStuffWorks.com, May 27, 2008. https://animals.howstuffworks.com/fish/sharks/electroreception.htm.

Court, Andrew. "Inventor of World's First Cellphone: Put Down Your Devices and 'Get a Life.'" *New York Post,* July 1, 2022. https://nypost.com/2022/07/01/inventor-of-worlds-first-cell-phone-put-down-your-devices.

Cross, Mrs. Andrew. "Science and Society in the Fifties." *Temple Bar: A London Magazine for Town and Country Readers* 93 (London: Richard Bentley & Son, 1891): 33–51.

Day, Anastasia. "The Titanic Connection." Hagley Museum website. https://www.hagley.org/librarynews/sarnoff/titanic-connection.

De Chair, Henry Graham. *Let Go Aft: The Indiscretions of a Salthorse.* Tunbridge Wells, England: Parapress LTD, 1993.

Deusner, Stephen. "'You Are My Sunshine': How a Maudlin Song Became a Children's Classic." Salon, May 26, 2013. https://www.salon.com/2013/05/26/you_are_my_sunshine_how_a_maudlin_song_became_a_childrens_classic.

Dibner, Bern. *Alessandro Volta and the Electric Battery.* New York: Franklin Watts, Inc., 1964.

Dingwall, John. "How a Trove of Letters Reveal the Secret (and Very Tangled) Life of the Scot who Downed the Luftwaffe." *The Sunday Post,* Glasgow, Scotland, October 1, 2019.

Dyson, Freeman J. "Why Is Maxwell's Theory So Hard to Understand?" *James Clerk Maxwell Commemorative Booklet.* Edinburgh, Scotland: James Clerk Maxwell Foundation, 1999.

Edwards, Steven A. "Heinrich Hertz and Electromagnetic Radiation." American Association for the Advancement of Science, October 12, 2012. https://www.aaas.org/heinrich-hertz-and-electromagnetic-radiation.

El-Akkad, Farah. "The Metropole Hotel: Living History." *Egypt Today,* April 16, 2017. https://www.egypttoday.com/Article/6/4021/The-Metropole-Hotel-Living-History.

Encyclopedia.com. "Radio 1929–1941." https://www.encyclopedia.com/education/news-and-education-magazines/radio-1929-1941.

———. "Turning Points: The Allies Begin to Win the War. https://www.encyclopedia.com/history/educational-magazines/turning-points-allies-begin-win-war.

Everitt, C. W. Francis. "Maxwell, Giant Shoulders to Stand Upon: A 'Mysteriously Prescient' Intellect." Review of *The Natural Philosophy of James Clerk Maxwell* by Peter M. Harman. *Physics Today* 52, no. 8 (August 1999): 61.

Fairweather, Cliff. *Hard Lying: The Story of the V&W Class Destroyers and the Men Who Sailed in Them.* Chelmsford, England: Avalon Associates, 2005.

Faraday, Michael. *The Chemical History of a Candle.* London: Chatto & Windus, 1908.

———. *Experimental Researches in Electricity,* vol.1. London: Richard and John Edward Taylor, 1839.

———. "Thoughts on Ray-Vibrations." *Philosophical Magazine and Journal of Science.* Series 3, Vol. 28, (May 1846).

Farago, Ladislas. *The Tenth Fleet: The True Story of the U.S. Navy's Phantom Fleet Battling U-Boats During World War II.* New York: Ivan Obolensky, Inc., 1962.

Federal Aviation Administration. "When Radar Came to Town." https://www.faa.gov/about/history/celebration/media/radar_departure_control.pdf.

Feynman, Richard, Robert Leighton, and Matthew Sands. *Feynman: The Feynman Lectures on Physics*, the New Millennium Edition. New York: Basic Books, 2011.

Fisher, David E. *A Summer Bright and Terrible: Winston Churchill, Lord Dowding, Radar, and the Impossible Triumph of the Battle of Britain*. Berkeley, CA: Shoemaker and Hoard, 2005.

Fisher, Howard J. *Faraday's Experimental Researches in Electricity: Guide to a First Reading*. Santa Fe, NM: Green Lion Press, 2001.

Forbes, Nancy, and Basil Mahon. *Faraday, Maxwell, and the Electromagnetic Field: How Two Men Revolutionized Physics*. Amherst, New York: Prometheus Books, 2014.

Francis, J. "Review of a Faraday Lecture Given at the Royal Institution, February 27, 1857." *The Athenaeum: Journal of Literature, Science, and the Fine Arts for the Year 1857*: 397–99.

Fuehrer Conferences on Naval Affairs 1939–1945. Annapolis, Maryland: Naval Institute Press, 1990.

Gannon, Michael. *Operation Drumbeat: The Dramatic True Story of Germany's U-Boat Attacks Along the American Coast in World War II*. New York: Harper and Row, 1990.

Goldstein, Richard. "Reinhard Hardegen, Who Led U-Boats to America's Shore, Dies at 105." *New York Times*, June 17, 2018.

Gregersen, Erik. "Alessandro Volta: Italian Scientist." *Encyclopedia Britannica*, December 12, 2022. https://www.britannica.com/biography/Alessandro-Volta.

Guerlac, Henry. *Radar in World War II*. Sections A–C. New York: American Institute of Physics, 1987.

Halpert, Julie Edelson. "Radar to Keep Drivers in Safe Lane." *Chicago Tribune*, October 30, 1994.

Hamilton, James. *A Life of Discovery: Michael Faraday, Giant of the Scientific Revolution*. New York: Random House, 2002.

Harman, P. M. *The Natural Philosophy of James Clerk Maxwell*. Cambridge, England: Cambridge University Press, 1998.

Helgason, Gudmundur, ed. "West Lashaway: American Steam Merchant." Uboat.net. https://uboat.net/allies/merchants/ship/2105.html.

Hilton, Stanley E. *Hitler's Secret War in South America 1939–1945: German Military Espionage and Allied Counterespionage in Brazil*. Baton Rouge, LA: Louisiana State University Press, 1981.

Hirshfeld, Alan. *The Electric Life of Michael Faraday*. New York: Walker & Company, 2006.

Hiskey, Daven. "The Microwave Oven Was Invented By Accident By a Man Who Was Orphaned and Never Finished Grammar School." *Today I Found Out* (blog), August 24, 2011. https://www.todayifoundout.com/index.php/2011/08/the-microwave-oven-was-invented-by-accident-by-a-man-who-was-orphaned-and-never-finished-grammar-school.

Hurd, Charles. "Two More Ships Torpedoed Off Coast, 46 Dead." *New York Times*, January 22, 1942.

James, Frank A. J. L., ed. *The Correspondence of Michael Faraday*, vols. 1–5. London: The Institution of Engineering and Technology, 1991–2008.

———. "The Tales of Benjamin Abbott: A Source for the Early Life of Michael Faraday." *The British Journal for the History of Science* 25, no. 2 (1992): 229–40.

James, William. "The Hidden Self." In *The Heart of William James*, 79–100. Edited by Robert Richardson. Cambridge, MA: Harvard University Press, 2010.

Jones, Bence. *The Life and Letters of Faraday in Two Volumes*. Philadelphia: J. B. Lippincott and Co., 1870.

Kahlbaum, Georg W. A., and Francis V. Darbishire, eds. *Letters of Faraday and Schoenbein, 1836–1862*. London: Williams and Norgate, 1899.

Kahn, E. J., Jr. "Annals of War and Peace: Hand to Hand." *The New Yorker*, February 8, 1988.

Kaiser, David. "From Blackboards to Bombs." *Nature*, July 30, 2015, 523–25.

Kantha, Sachi Sri. "Why Wright Brothers Failed to Receive Nobel Prize Recognition?" *Current Science* 103, no. 4 (August 25, 2012): 435–37.

Kinsey, Gordon. *Orfordness: Secret Site*. Lavenham, England: Terence Dalton Limited, 1981.

Kuhn, Ferdinand, Jr. "Kennedy Says U.S. War Policy Rests on Our National Interest." *New York Times*, March 19, 1938.

Lazarus, M. J. *IEE Proceedings*. 133, no. 2 (1986): 109–18.

Legacy.com. Robert Bell Obituary. 2014. https://www.legacy.com/us/obituaries/heraldtribune/name/robert-bell-obituary?id=9326721.

Loewenheim, Francis L., Harold D. Langley, and Manfred Jonas, eds. *Roosevelt and Churchill: Their Secret Wartime Correspondence*. New York: Saturday Review Press/E. Dutton & Co. Inc., 1975.

Lovell, Sir Bernard. *Echoes of War: The Story of H2S Radar*. Bristol, England: Adam Hilger, 1991.

Lyons, Louis M. "Kennedy Says Democracy All Done." *Boston Globe*, November 10, 1940.

Martin, Thomas, ed. *Faraday's Diary, Being the Various Philosophical Notes of Experimental Investigation*. London: Bell and Sons, 1932–1936.

Mertes, Alyssa. "The History of Sunscreen: When Was It Invented & By Who?" *Quality Logo Products Blog*, November 29, 2022. https://www.qualitylogoproducts.com/blog/history-of-sunscreen.

Moore, John Hammond. *The Faustball Tunnel: German POWs in America and Their Great Escape*. New York: Random House, 1978.

Morison, Samuel Eliot. *The Battle of the Atlantic, September 1939–1943: History of United States Naval Operations in World War II*, Vol. 1. Boston: Little, Brown and Company, 1960.

Moss, John. "An Inductive Genius." *New Scientist* 92, no. 1278, November 5, 1981, 393–94.

National Archives. "From Benjamin Franklin to James Bowdoin, 24 January 1752." Founders Online. https://founders.archives.gov/documents/Franklin/01-04-02-0085.

National Archives. "Post Mortems on Enemy Submarines, Office of Naval Intelligence, 250-G, Serial No. 5. Sinking of U-162." September 5, 1942.

New York Times. "Sunscreen: A History." June 24, 2010. https://www.nytimes.com/2010/06/24/fashion/24skinside.html.

———. "Third Ship Torpedoed Off the Atlantic Coast." January 19, 1942.

———. "U-Boats Off Coast Hit 4th Ship After 22 Die in Blazing Tanker." January 20, 1942.

———. "U-Boat Torpedoes Norse Tanker Off Jersey." January 26, 1942.

Nirenberg, David, and Ricardo L. Nirenberg. *Uncountable: A Philosophical History of Number and Humanity from Antiquity to the Present.* Chicago: University of Chicago Press, 2021.

Offley, Ed. *The Burning Shore: How Hitler's U-Boats Brought World War II to America.* New York: Basic Books, 2014.

Padfield, Peter. *Dönitz: The Last Führer.* New York: Harper & Row, Publishers, 1984.

Page, John R. "Little Known Facts About Dr. Robert M. Page." *RF Cafe: Tech News, Resources & Entertainment,* February 18, 2019. https://www.rfcafe.com/miscellany/smorgasbord/robert-page-pulse-radar-history-kirts-cogitation-310.htm.htm.

Page, Robert Morris. *The Origin of Radar: An Epic of Modern Technology.* Garden City, New York: Anchor Books, 1962.

Palmer, Brian. "How Much Ivory Is in the Ivory Coast?" *Slate,* April 6, 2011. https://slate.com/news-and-politics/2011/04/how-much-ivory-is-in-the-ivory-coast.html.

Paone, Thomas. "K Ships vs. U-Boats." Smithsonian National Air and Space Museum website, July 8, 2020. https://airandspace.si.edu/stories/editorial/k-ships-vs-u-boats.

Pavlovich, Lou Jr. "Baseball's Great Inventor of All Times." *Collegiate Baseball,* January 6, 2012. http://baseballnews.com/old/features/stories/baseballs_great_inventor_of_all_time.htm.

Plageman, Nate. *Highlife Saturday Night: Popular Music and Social Change in Urban Ghana.* Bloomington, IN: Indiana University Press, 2013.

Potamian, Brother, and James J. Walsh. *Makers of Electricity.* New York: Fordham University Press, 1909.

Quote Park. "Isaac Newton." https://quotepark.com/quotes/1857712-isaac-newton-god-created-everything-by-number-weight-and-measure.

Randall, J. T. "Radar and the Magnetron." *Journal of the Royal Society of Arts* 94, no. 4715 (April 12, 1946): 302–23.

Raboy, Marc. *Marconi: The Man Who Networked the World.* New York: Oxford University Press, 2016.

Richmond Times-Dispatch. "Navy Needs Operators for 'Radar.'" December 24, 1941.

Roper & Sons Funeral Home. "Obituary: Mary Ruth Whitbeck." February 23, 2019. https://www.roperandsons.com/obit/mary-ruth-whitbeck.

Roskill, Stephen. *Churchill and the Admirals.* Barnsley, Great Britain: Pen & Sword Military Classics, 1977.

Royal Air Force Museum. "Battle of the Nations." https://www.rafmuseum.org.uk/research/online-exhibitions/history-of-the-battle-of-britain/battle-of-the-nations.

Royal Society. "History of the Royal Society." https://royalsociety.org/about-us/history.

Royal Society of Publishing. "On the Electricity Excited by the Mere Contact of Conducting Substances of Different Kinds." In a Letter from Mr. Alexander Volta, F.R.S. Professor of Natural Philosophy in the University of Pavia, to the Rt. Hon. Sir Joseph Banks. Read June 26, 1800. https://royalsocietypublishing.org/doi/pdf/10.1098/rspl.1800.0016.

Runbeck, Margaret Lee. "A Friend of a Friend of His." *Good Housekeeping,* August 1943, 35, 177–82.

Sacks, Oliver. *Uncle Tungsten: Memoirs of a Chemical Boyhood.* New York: Random House, 2002.

SeaLevelRise.org. "America's Sea Level Has Risen by 6.5 Inches Since 1950." https://sealevelrise.org, 2023.

Secor, H. Winfield. "Tesla's Views on Electricity and the War." *The Electrical Experimenter,* August 1917.

Segre, Emilio. *From Falling Bodies to Radio Waves: Classical Physicists and Their Discoveries.* Mineola, New York: Dover Publications, Inc., 1984.

Shaw, Richard. "Richard Shaw's Story" in *Adrift: The Story of Twenty Days on a Raft in the South Atlantic.* New York: Evangelical Publishers, 1943, 120–25.

Skulls in the Stars (blog). "The Birth of Electromagnetism (1820)." April 3, 2011. https://skullsinthestars.com/2011/04/03/the-birth-of-electromagnetism-1820.

Spirit of St. Louis 2 Project. "Charles Lindbergh, An American Aviator: Des Moines Speech: Delivered in Des Moines, Iowa, on September 11, 1941, This Speech was Met with Outrage in Many Quarters." http://www.charleslindbergh.com/americanfirst/speech.asp.

Stauffer, Robert C. "Speculation and Experiment in the Background of Oersted's Discovery of Electromagnetism." *Isis* 48, no. 1 (March 1957): 33–50.

Stephens, Donna Lampkin. "God Does Protect His Children." *501 Life,* July 21, 2012.

Stewart, Doug "The Doc." "Heinrich Hertz." Famous Scientists, November 23, 2015. https://www.famousscientists.org/heinrich-hertz.

StudyCountry.com. "A Short History of Cote D'Ivoire." https://www.studycountry.com/guide/CI-history.htm.

Syrett, David, ed. *The Battle of the Atlantic and Signals Intelligence: U-Boat Situations and Trends, 1941–1945.* Brookfield, VT: Ashgate, 1998.

Tesla, Nikola, as told to Alfred Albelli. "Radio Power Will Revolutionize the World." *Modern Mechanix and Inventions*, July 1934, 40–42, 117–19.

Taylor, Hoyt. *Radio Reminiscences: A Half Century*. Washington, DC: Naval Research Laboratory, 1960.

Thompson, Silvanus Phillips. *Michael Faraday, His Life and Work*. New York: Macmillan Company, 1898.

Torchinsky, Jason. "I Had No Idea the Renault Fuego Was the Car with This Huge Automotive First." *Jalopnik*, February 23, 2021. https://jalopnik. com/i-had-no-idea-the-renault-fuego-was-the-car-with-this-h-1846330434.

Tretkoff, Ernie. "March 20, 1800: Volta describes the Electric Battery." APS News, March 2006. https:// www.aps,org/publications/apsnews/200603/ history.cfm.

Turner, Richard L. "U.S. Declares War on All Axis Powers." *Democrat and Chronicle*, December 12, 1941.

Tzu, Sun. *The Art of War*. Translated by Lionel Giles. http://classics.mit.edu/Tzu/artwar.html.

U-Boat Archive. "Action Reports from Quentin, Vimy, Pathfinder, and Pathfinder Report Covering the Action Against U-162." http://www.uboatarchive. net/U-162A/U-162PathfinderReport.htm.

———. "HMS Vimy." https://uboat.net/allies/ warships/ship/5454.html.

———. "Report on the Interrogation of Survivors from U-162 Sunk on September 3, 1942." https://www. uboatarchive.net/U-162A/U-162INT.htm.

———. "Ships Hit by U-boats: Sir Huon: Panamanian Motor Merchant." https://uboat.net/allies/ merchants/ship/2106.html.

———. "Ships Hit by U-boats: Topa Topa: American Steam Merchant." https://uboat.net/allies/ merchants/ship/2104.html.

———. "U-66: 6th War Period." https://uboatarchive. net/U-66/KTB66-6.htm.

Venables, Raymond Briggs and Richard McDonough, recorder. "Raymond Briggs Venables: Oral History." Imperial War Museum, London, Catalogue #21552, Reel 10. https://www.iwm.org.uk/collections/item/ object/80022193.

University of Virginia Miller Center. "December 11, 1941: Message to Congress Requesting War Declarations with Germany and Italy." Presidential Speeches, Franklin D. Roosevelt. https://millercenter.org/the-presidency/presidential-speeches/december-11-1941-message-congress-requesting-war-declarations.

Voss, David, ed. "This Month in Physics History: December 17, 1902: First Radio Message to Cross the Atlantic from North America." American Physical Society, December 2019. https://www.aps. org/publications/apsnews/201911/history.cfm.

Watson-Watt, Robert. *The Pulse of Radar*. New York: Dial Press, 1959.

———. *Three Steps to Victory: A Personal Account by Radar's Greatest Pioneer*. London: Odhams Press Limited, 1957.

Whistler, Simon, host. "Michael Faraday: The Father of Electricity." Stitcher. *Biographics: History One Life at a Time*, ep. 333, August 13, 2020. https://www. stitcher.com/show/biographics-history-one-life-at-a-time/episode/333-michael-faraday-the-father-of-electricity-76933696.

Whitbeck, Mary. "A Rainbow Every Day: A Woman, Four Kids and 12 Sailors Adrift in the Atlantic." December 2006. *Alliance Life*. https://legacy. cmalliance.org/alife/a-rainbow-every-day.

———. "A Rainbow Every Day—Part Two: The Journey Toward Land Continues." January 2007. *Alliance Life*. https://legacy.cmalliance.org/ alife/a-rainbow-every-day-part-two/.

Whittaker, E. T. *A History of the Theories of Aether and Electricity: From the Age of Descartes to the End of the Nineteenth Century*. London: Longmans, Green, and Co., 1910.

Wickman, Forrest. "This Party's Blowin' Up: Why Do We Celebrate with Balloons?" *Slate*, December 13, 2011. https://slate.com/human-interest/2011/12/ party-balloons-a-history.html.

Wikipedia. "Flight of the Norwegian National Treasury." https://en.wikipedia.org/wiki/Flight_of_the_ Norwegian_National_Treasury.

———. "Ivory Coast." https://en.wikipedia.org/wiki/ Ivory_Coast.

———. "Makola Market." https://en.wikipedia.org/ wiki/Makola_Market.

———. "Naval Base Trinidad." https://en.wikipedia. org/wiki/Naval_Base_Trinidad.

———. "Pemmican." https://en.wikipedia.org/wiki/ Pemmican.

———. "Pilot fish." https://en.wikipedia.org/wiki/ Pilot_fish.

———. "*Sonderkommando Blaich*." https://en. wikipedia.org/wiki/Sonderkommando_Blaich.

Wilkins, M. H. F. "John Turton Randall (23 March 1905–16 June 1984)." *Biographical Memoirs of Fellows of the Royal Society* 33, 1987, 493–535.

Wu, Chau H. "Electric Fish and the Discovery of Animal Electricity: The Mystery of the Electric Fish Motivated Research into Electricity and Was Instrumental in the Emergence of Electrophysiology." *American Scientist* 72, no. 6 (November–December 1984): 598–607.

Wylie, Philip, and Laurence Schwab. "The Battle of Florida." *The Saturday Evening Post*, March 11, 1944, 14–15, 52–58.

IMAGE CREDITS

Sidebar Backgrounds
Adobe Stock, digital scrapbooking kit: aged paper, by Anja Kaiser (file #34624706): pages 2, 9, 12, 20/21, 27, 28, 35, 38, 45, 51, 56/57, 65, 70, 73, 87, 90, 95, 106, 111, 112/113, 124/125, 127, 132, 138, 155, 158

Chapter 1
Wikimedia Commons, Cunard Line postcard of the RMS *Laconia* circa 1921: page 7
Library of Congress, Prints and Photographs Division (LCCN: 2004681916): page 8
Library of Congress, Newspaper (LCCN: sn8304599): page 13

Chapter 2
Wikimedia Commons, Pan Am Boeing 307 Stratocruiser "Clipper Rainbow": pages 18–19
National Archives Foundation, from the Records of the US Information Agency, Accra, Ghana: page 20

Chapter 3
Wikimedia Commons, Luigi Galvani's monument, Piazza Galvani, Bologna, Italy: page 22 (main image)
Wikimedia Commons, Luigi Galvani's frog legs: page 22 (overlay image)
Wellcome Collection, original Voltaic pile: page 26
Wikimedia Commons, Oersted's experiment: page 29

Chapter 4
Wikimedia Commons, SS *West Lashaway* shortly after launch on 12 September 1918 and before completion of her superstructure: page 32
New York World Telegram, front page January 19, 1942: page 36

Chapter 5
Wikimedia Commons, photo of painting of Michael Faraday by Thomas Phillips, 1842: page 40 (main image)
Wikimedia Commons, drawing of Michael Faraday's experiment demonstrating electromagnetic rotation: page 40 (overlay image)
Wikimedia Commons, Professor Faraday lecturing at the Royal Institution from the *Illustrated London News*, 16 February 1856: page 46
Wikimedia Commons, drawing of Faraday disk, 1884: page 49

Chapter 6
Wikipedia, U-66 on 7 August 1943: page 60
Wikimedia Commons, photograph of pemmican ball, Jen Arrr, 13 January 2017: page 65

Chapter 7
Wikimedia Commons, James Clerk Maxwell: page 68 (main image)
Wikimedia Commons, the first spark-gap transmitter of Hertz: page 75
Wikimedia Commons, re-creation of the first radio transmitter: page 77
Wikimedia Commons, last lifeboat successfully launched from the *Titanic*, J. W. Barker: page 78

Chapter 9
Wikimedia Commons, photograph of Nikola Tesla at age 34, circa 1890: page 92 (main image)
Adobe Stock, silhouette of thunderstorm lightning by vertyr (file #42650881): page 92 (overlay image)
Naval History and Heritage Command, USS *New York* (catalog #NH77350): page 105

Chapter 11
Wikimedia Commons, cavity magnetron, National Electronics Museum: page 120 (main image)

Chapter 12
Adobe Stock, ocean storm by Nejron Photo (file #27502438): page 130
Wikimedia Commons, *Naucrates ductor* (pilot fish): page 131

Chapter 13
V & W Destroyer Association, Peter McQuade, photographer unknown: page 134 (main image)
V & W Destroyer Association, Peter McQuade, photographer unknown: page 144

Chapter 15
The New York Public Library Digital Collections, Milestones in National Service: An Advertisement of the American Telephone and Telegraph Company: page 156 (main image)
Adobe Stock, Evolution of Phone by MoreVector (file #102858519): page 156 (overlay image)
Wikimedia Commons, radar gun used by the police: page 159
PublicDomainFiles.com, MRI machine: page 160

INDEX